Easy MIX&MATCH

Machine Paper Piecing

70 Quilt Blocks for Foundation Piecing

CAROL DOAK

That Patchwork Place®

Credits

Editor-in-Chief .... Barbara Weiland
Technical Editor .... Sally Schneider
Managing Editor .... Greg Sharp
Copy Editor .... Tina Cook
Proofreader .... Leslie Phillips
Design Director .... Judy Petry
Text and Cover Designer .... Cheryl Stevenson
Production Assistant .... Claudia L'Heureux
Illustrator .... Carolyn Kraft
Illustration Assistant .... Lisa McKenney
Photographer .... Brent Kane

Easy Mix & Match Machine Paper Piecing
© 1995 by Carol Doak
That Patchwork Place, Inc., PO Box 118, Bothell, WA
98041-0118 USA

Printed in the United States of America
00 99 98 97 96 95   6 5 4 3 2 1

Library of Congress Cataloging-in-Publication Data

Doak, Carol,
    Easy mix & match machine paper piecing : 70 quilt blocks for foundation piecing / Carol Doak.
        p.   cm.
    ISBN 1-56477-128-8
    1. Patchwork—Patterns. 2. Machine quilting. 3. Patchwork quilts. I. Title.
TT835.D612   1995
746.46—dc20   95-18306
                                                CIP

Acknowledgments

My heartfelt thanks and appreciation go to:
    Sherry Reis, Pam Ludwig, Ginny Guaraldi, Terry Maddox, Susan Raban, Ellen Peters, Helen Weinman, and B. J. Berlo for sharing my enthusiasm for machine paper piecing and their wonderful quilts;
    Judith Siccama, Mary Golden, Faye Labanaris, Donna Slusser, Pat Magaret, Mary Hickey, Joan Hanson, Doreen Burbank, Sandra Hatch, and Mary Stori for their friendship and for making quiltmaking a wonderful sharing art form;
    Barbara Weiland, Ursula Reikes, Marion Shelton, Sally Schneider, and the entire staff at That Patchwork Place for always being there with their support, expertise, and friendship.

Dedication

To Marion Shelton, a very dear and special lady who lives life with such grace.

MISSION STATEMENT

WE ARE DEDICATED TO PROVIDING QUALITY PRODUCTS THAT ENCOURAGE CREATIVITY AND PROMOTE SELF-ESTEEM IN OUR CUSTOMERS AND OUR EMPLOYEES.

WE STRIVE TO MAKE A DIFFERENCE IN THE LIVES WE TOUCH.

That Patchwork Place is an employee-owned, financially secure company.

Contents

Preface

While preparing the paper-pieced blocks for *Easy Machine Paper Piecing, Easy Reversible Vests,* and *Easy Paper-Pieced Keepsake Quilts,* I played with several design exercises that I wanted to explore further. First I experimented with block combinations. I discovered that delightful designs developed when I combined and rotated four blocks with diagonal designs. The result was a single new design with a central focus and an intricate radiating quality.

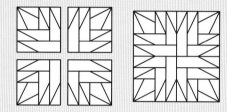

To expand upon the concept, I designed blocks that continued this diagonal arrangement through the block. When I combined these blocks and rotated them, I often found a surprising secondary design.

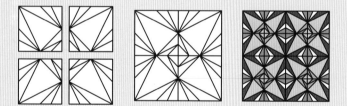

The second design exercise I explored was the use of two-section blocks. Design options increased when I broke a block into two paper-pieced sections. With two sections, I could construct blocks that had previously been impossible to paper-piece because of the manner in which seams intersected. In some instances these sections could be assembled in a different order or interchanged with similar sectional blocks to create even more designs.

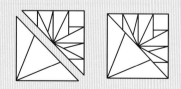

Two sections permit more designs.

Original design

New design created
by assembling the sections
in an alternate fashion

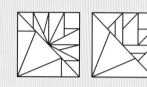

Original block designs

New designs created
by interchanging
the bottom sections

The third design exercise I investigated was the creation of a single new block from separate block units. For example, flower-top units and stem/leaf units can be combined to create a variety of flower designs.

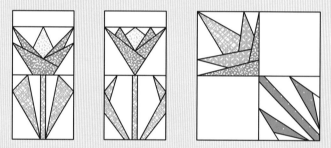

This book contains blocks that are the result of exploring paper-piecing options. Mixing and matching these blocks yields almost unlimited design possibilities. The "Gallery of Quilts" on pages 81–88 shows some of the options, but these quilts only scratch the surface of the many opportunities that await when you play with these new paper-pieced block designs.

In addition to mixing and matching the blocks in this book, you can also combine these new designs with those previously published in *Easy Machine Paper Piecing, Easy Reversible Vests,* and *Easy Paper-Pieced Keepsake Quilts.*

One of my greatest joys is seeing the exciting patchwork projects that result from the books I have written. I can hardly wait to see the quilts that are the product of your creativity and these new mix-and-match blocks for paper piecing!

Introduction

This book follows the same format as *Easy Machine Paper Piecing* and *Easy Paper-Pieced Keepsake Quilts,* so you will feel comfortable right from the start with these new designs.

Paper-pieced patchwork blocks are created by machine-stitching oversized fabric pieces to a paper foundation in a numbered sequence. The paper provides a stable base, allowing extreme accuracy even when piecing the tiniest pieces and the sharpest points. Because you utilize a paper foundation, you can also include fabrics not normally used in patchwork, such as knits, lamés, and silks. These fabrics can add a very special touch.

Paper-pieced patchwork blocks are quick and easy to produce. With no templates to make or fabric to mark, you go right to your sewing machine and begin stitching blocks. There is no high degree of skill needed to make intricate patchwork designs. If you can machine-sew a straight line, you can create paper-pieced patchwork. I jokingly tell new students in my paper-piecing workshops that they are as good at paper piecing on that day as they are going to get. They will become more proficient at cutting the fabric pieces and faster at placing the fabric and sewing the lines, but their paper-pieced patchwork blocks are accurate from the first one they make.

The blocks are presented in a 4" size so that you can combine them with the block designs previously published in *Easy Machine Paper Piecing* and *Easy Paper-Pieced Keepsake Quilts.* You can reduce or enlarge them on a photocopy machine to make quilt projects in a variety of sizes. You can also use them with the 3" block designs presented in *Easy Reversible Vests.*

The beginning sections explain how to cut the fabric pieces and how to sew the fabric to the paper foundation. The block designs are grouped in categories. Each category is numbered sequentially, and the block numbers continue the numbering sequence begun in my other books on paper piecing. The "Block and Quilt Design Possibilities" section explores the many design options that are available when you combine these blocks.

I hope you have fun exploring the possibilities as you create your own special paper-pieced quilts.

Working with Block Designs

The 4" piecing foundations in this book are full size and ready to use. The pieces are numbered to indicate the stitching sequence. Sew the seam between piece #1 and piece #2 first, and then the remaining seams in order. A few of the block designs require a unit with one or two prepieced seams. These pieced units are identified on the block pattern with a "//" through the seam and are explained in greater detail on pages 14–15. Some of the blocks are two-section blocks. Piece each unit separately, then join them to form the block. This procedure is described on page 14.

Reproducing Block Designs

There are two ways to reproduce the blocks. You may trace them on tracing paper, or you may photocopy them. The photocopy machine is particularly useful if you need to reduce or enlarge designs to fit your particular project.

Tracing

Place a piece of transparent tracing paper on top of the 4" block design and secure with removable tape to keep the paper from shifting while you draw. (See page 13 for more information on removable tape.) Using a ruler and a mechanical pencil, trace the lines, markings, and numbers. Make a separate tracing for each block required.

Although tracing the blocks by hand takes more time than photocopying, it does offer advantages. The lines are easier to see during the design and sewing process, and the method lends itself to spontaneity, since you don't need to use a photocopy machine that might not be available the moment you want to sew a block.

Photocopying

You can use a photocopy machine to reproduce block designs; however, photocopy machines do produce copies with slight variances. The photocopy of a 4" block may be just a hair larger (less than 1%) than the original, and the blocks can be ever so slightly off square. While a perfect square has identical diagonal measurements from corner to corner, a photocopy can have a variance of approximately ¹⁄₁₆". This variance is so slight and occurs over such a great distance that normally you cannot see it. *It is not advisable to make a copy from a copy,* because doing so compounds the variance. Be sure to make copies for each quilt on the same machine, using the original block design as the master. Different photocopy machines may produce copies with different variances. Always check to see that the photocopied blocks are the correct size for the intended project. Use a rotary cutter and a square plastic ruler to trim photocopies ½" away from the outside finished block lines on all sides. Trim ¼" away from the joining seam of two-section blocks.

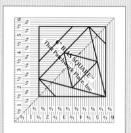

Enlarging and Reducing Block Designs

You can enlarge and reduce the 4" block designs with a photocopy machine. After much experimentation, I have come to the conclusion that all enlargements and reductions for a chosen design should be made from the original patterns on the same photocopy machine. On most commercial photocopy machines, you can reduce copies to 64% and enlarge them to 156%. The same variance applies to blocks that you enlarge or reduce. You cannot enlarge a block larger than 6", however, without making a copy from an enlarged copy, where the variance is already present. I don't recommend making copies of copies, because the variance becomes greater with each generation of photocopies. Below is a list of the common proportions needed to enlarge or reduce the block designs in this book.

Original Size	Desired Size	Proportion Change
4"	3"	Reduce 75%
4"	5"	Enlarge 125%
4"	6"	Enlarge 150%
3"*	4"	Enlarge 133%

*There are many 3" blocks in Easy Reversible Vests.

You can easily calculate any other required changes with a Proportional Scale. This tool comes in handy when calculating the necessary percentage of the original to reduce or enlarge. Align the size of the original block on the inner wheel with the desired size of the

reduction or enlargement on the outer wheel. The percentage of reduction or enlargement appears in the window. This is a great little visual tool for those who prefer not to make calculations!

Symmetrical and Asymmetrical Blocks

The 4" block design patterns in this book represent the wrong side of the block. In a symmetrical design, the fabric side of the block design is the same as the marked side of the block. In an asymmetrical design, the fabric side of the block is the reverse of the marked side of the block. Use the block-front drawings and the color photographs to see how the blocks will appear from the front once they are pieced.

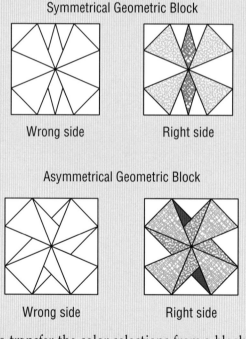

Symmetrical Geometric Block

Wrong side   Right side

Asymmetrical Geometric Block

Wrong side   Right side

To transfer the color selections from a block-front drawing to a foundation, indicate your color choices on the *blank* side of the paper design so that they correspond with the finished color example.

If you trace the blocks onto tracing paper, the lines are easy to see. If you photocopy the blocks, the lines should be dark enough to see from the unmarked side when the paper is placed on a white surface. If you cannot see the lines, simply place a light source beneath the block so they are more visible.

Creating the Reverse of a Block Design

There may be times when you want to make the reverse of a block. Perhaps you would like to have your cats facing in opposite directions. If you use piecing foundations marked on tracing paper, simply place the fabric pieces on the side with the pencil lines to create the reverse of the design. The tracing paper should be translucent enough to see through to the sewing lines. If you use the photocopy machine to reproduce your reverse blocks, first trace the design on tracing paper with a dark pencil. Then turn it over, retrace the lines, and mark the numbers on that side of the tracing paper. Mark the numbered side "Reverse" so that you won't be confused later. Copy the "Reverse" design for your paper patterns.

Cat block   The reverse of the Cat block

Cutting Fabric Pieces to Approximate Size

To cut fabric the approximate size for the intended area, take a quick measurement of the space with a ruler and add a total of ¾" to 1". You must cut pieces a bit larger than necessary, allowing more than the customary ¼"-wide seam allowance. Trim excess fabric ¼" away from seams either before or after you sew the adjoining seams. Since the line drawing being measured is the wrong side of the block, *always cut the fabric with the wrong side facing you.* Because fabric strips are easy to measure and place accurately, I tend to cut them the finished size plus ½" for seam allowances. Fill in unusual shapes with oversize rectangles or squares. It is not necessary to cut the exact shape. Remember, when dealing with angled seams and odd shapes, bigger is always better.

Before attaching these odd shapes, place the fabric piece right side up on the blank side of the block, over the intended area. Hold the marked side of the foundation up to a light source and check to see that the fabric piece is large enough to fill the intended area plus a generous seam allowance all the way around. When you are sure that the fabric is the proper size, simply flip the piece over along the seam to be sewn and position the cut edge of the fabric ¼" away from the seam line.

Fabric Grain Options

Fabric has three grains: lengthwise, crosswise, and bias. The lengthwise grain has the least amount of stretch and runs parallel to the selvages. The crosswise grain runs from selvage to selvage and has a bit of stretch. Both the lengthwise and crosswise grains are considered the straight grain of the fabric. The bias runs diagonally through the fabric and has the greatest amount of stretch.

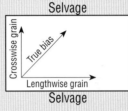

Because you sew the fabric pieces to a paper foundation, you can place the fabric on the foundation without regard to the direction of the fabric grain. However, there will be occasions when you do want to place the fabric pieces on the foundation so they open with the straight of grain running vertically and horizontally through the block. There are three choices for fabric-grain placement when piecing on paper foundations: random-grain placement, straight-grain placement, or a combination of both.

Using Random-Grain Placement

In this placement, the fabric pieces are sewn without attention to the direction of the fabric grain along the sewing edge. This results in random-grain placement when the piece is sewn and opened. Paper piecing permits this type of construction because the paper provides the stability necessary to prevent the pieces from stretching as you sew them. However, bias edges along the edge of a block will stretch once the paper is removed. For this reason, I don't recommend using random-grain placement for block pieces that will be placed at the outside edge of a project. It is also why I suggest that you do not remove the paper until the blocks have been joined to other blocks and/or borders.

Large pieces of fabric and directional-print fabrics used with random-grain placement can be distracting. Since fabric grain is more apparent in solid fabrics, use tiny-scale prints in place of solids, especially in large areas. This helps to camouflage grain direction.

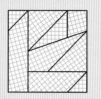

Random-grain placement

Using Straight-Grain Placement

Fabric pieces in this arrangement are sewn so that the straight of grain runs vertically and horizontally through the block. This placement is important for block pieces that are used at the outside edges of a project, when directional prints are used, and when the fabric pieces are large enough to make the fabric grain noticeable.

Straight-grain placement

The direction of the seam line to be sewn, rather than the shape of the piece to be added, determines how you should cut each piece of fabric so it opens on the straight of grain.

Vertical and Horizontal Seam Lines

The lower section of the Flower block below is an example of a design that contains only vertical and horizontal lines. All the strips should be cut on the straight grain of the fabric and then placed on the vertical and horizontal seam lines.

Straight-grain placement
on vertical and horizontal lines

Diagonal Seam Lines

Fabrics that will be used on diagonal seam lines should be on the bias so that the vertical and horizontal sides of the block will both be on the straight of grain. In the block below, the sewn edges of the highlighted pieces are cut on the bias.

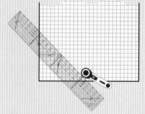

The joining edges of these pieces are cut along the bias grain of the fabric.

To cut fabric on the bias, cut strips diagonally at a 45° angle.

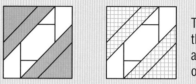

Sewing "Weird"-Angle Seam Lines

I use the term "weird" for any seam line that is not horizontal, vertical, or at a 45° angle. I use this term only because it is not necessary to know what the angle is, only how to cut the fabric so that it ends up on the straight of grain once it has been sewn and opened. Use the following method to cut weird angles so they will finish on the straight of grain:

1. Place the block design on the cutting mat.
2. Place a long rotary ruler along the seam line you are about to sew—the weird angle.
3. Place the fabric you intend to add, wrong side up, either above or below the block and under the extending end of the ruler. Make sure the straight of grain runs vertically and horizontally. Cut along the angle with a rotary cutter.

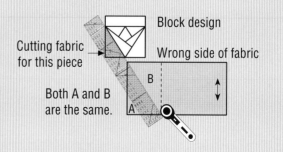

Block design

Cutting fabric for this piece

Wrong side of fabric

Both A and B are the same.

4. Place the cut edge of the fabric along the seam. Sew in place and open.

■ **Tip:** To avoid confusion, cut weird angles as needed. I like to make a small pencil mark on the paper block of the weird-angle line I just cut so I don't forget.

To cut the reverse of the same weird angle, fold the fabric right sides together and cut both layers at the same time. When cutting bias pieces and weird angles, bigger is better. Oversize pieces ensure that the fabric will fill the intended area once it is sewn and opened. You can always trim the excess fabric after sewing the adjoining pieces.

If you are making multiples of the same block design, use the cut fabric as a template to cut additional pieces. Use two strips, placed right sides together, to cut the reverse pieces at the same time.

When the first piece of a block contains weird angles, simply pin the piece right side up with the straight of grain running vertically and horizontally.

Placing Fabric Strips

Several block designs utilize strips of fabric. Use straight-of-grain strips when the strips are set vertically or horizontally in the block. You can also use straight-of-grain strips along diagonal seams if you piece with random-grain placement. Cut bias strips for diagonally placed strips so that outside edges will finish on the straight of grain.

You can precut a supply of fabric strips on the bias or on the straight of grain. They should measure the finished width plus ½" for seam allowances. Add straight-grain fabric strips to any of the paper-piecing foundations to enlarge them or to stabilize the outside edges where you used random-grain fabric placement.

Deal with fabric grain on a block-by-block basis at first, and it will soon become second nature.

Quilt Blocks

This section contains step-by-step directions for paper piecing blocks by machine. There is much more information presented than you need to get started. Since the best way to learn is by doing, begin by piecing small blocks with random-grain placement to practice the mechanics of cutting and sewing the fabric pieces. Then move on to the larger blocks and straight-grain

placement. As you create the blocks, the techniques will become routine. When you need a refresher, you can always refer to this section in the book.

Getting Ready to Sew

When I begin a project, I like to set the stage so that I have everything I need ready and available. Getting up and down for forgotten items may provide exercise, but it slows your progress.

- Make sure that your sewing machine is in good working order and sews a good straight stitch.
- Set the stitch length on the machine for approximately 18 to 20 stitches per inch, and use a size 90/14 needle. A short stitch length and a larger needle perforate the paper better, making it easier to tear the paper away later.
- Select a sewing thread that blends with most of the fabrics used. I rely on white, gray, or black for most blocks.
- Create a pressing and cutting area next to the machine by lowering the ironing board to sewing level. Use one end to cut and the other end to press. If you use photocopies, place a piece of muslin on your ironing board to protect it from possible ink transfer.
- Have a pair of sharp, small scissors on hand to trim the fabric pieces before and after sewing them.
- Have your rotary cutter, plastic ruler, and mat close at hand. Choose the ruler size based on the size of the blocks being made. For the 4" piecing foundations, a 6" square ruler works fine.
- Have your "unsewing" tool (seam ripper) handy just on the outside chance that a quick take-out maneuver becomes necessary.
- If you rely upon seeing through previous pieces of fabric to place subsequent pieces (rather than using the alternative method described on page 12), set up a small lamp near the sewing machine. Generally, the placement of the first piece is easy to see without a light source. However, to properly place succeeding pieces of fabric, you need to be able to see through the previous pieces of untrimmed fabric.
- Last, but probably most important, select your fabric. Remember, the unmarked side of the block is the fabric side. To avoid confusion, always note your fabric choices on the unmarked side of the block design.

■ Tip: When using larger pieces of fabric (rather than scraps), cut strips approximately 6" wide; then, cut smaller pieces from the strips as needed. This makes the fabric more manageable and the sewing area less cluttered.

You are now ready to paper piece your first block. Although this may be an unfamiliar piecing method, it does not rely upon acquired skills for success. Simply follow the step-by-step procedure to make perfect patchwork blocks.

Step-by-Step Sewing Procedure

1. Place the fabric for piece #1 right side up on the unmarked side of the paper; pin in place. Make sure piece #1 covers the area marked 1 and extends a generous ¼" on all sides. You can cut the piece larger than needed and trim the excess fabric after sewing the adjoining seams. Once you have sewn a few blocks, you may want to just hold the first piece in position and eliminate the pin. If you use copy paper, hold the paper up to a light source with the marked side of the block toward you to facilitate proper placement.

2. With the wrong side of the fabric facing you, cut the approximate size for piece #2. Remember, the marked side of the block is the wrong side of the block. Place piece #2 on top of piece #1, right sides together, along the joining seam line. Make sure both fabrics extend at least ¼" beyond the seam lines. Don't concern yourself with an exact ¼"-wide seam allowance. You can trim any excess seam allowance after sewing the seam. However, you do want to keep the edge of piece #2 parallel to the seam line to keep the grain true.

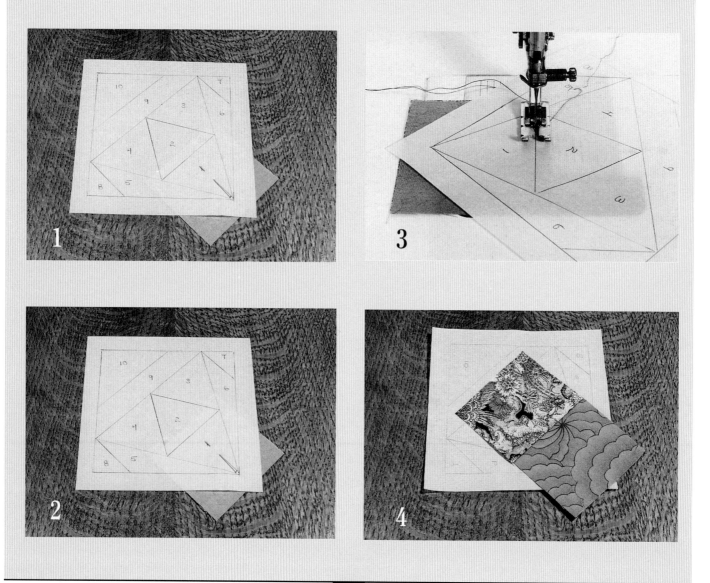

■ **Tip:** Check to make sure the piece is placed correctly and is large enough by pinching the seam-allowance edge and opening piece #2 to see if it covers the intended area plus seam allowances.

3. Holding the fabrics in position, place the paper block, marked side up, under the presser foot. Sew the first seam line between pieces #1 and #2. Extend the stitching a few stitches beyond the beginning and end of the line.

4. Trim away any excess fabric in the seam allowance to ¼". Open piece #2 and finger-press by running your fingers across the seam. Press with a dry iron on a cotton setting.

5. Add piece #3 to piece #2. Use a light source to check that the edge of piece #3 extends at least ¼" beyond the seam lines. Sew the second seam line between piece #2 and piece #3. Press.

6. Continue in the same manner, adding the remaining pieces in numerical order.

7. Using a rotary cutter and ruler, trim the edges of the block, leaving a ¼"-wide seam allowance beyond the outside lines of the marked design. If the ruler slips on the paper, apply small circular stick-on tabs of sandpaper to the ruler to stabilize it.

No matter how many pieces a block design has, the construction is the same. Always add pieces in numerical order until the design is complete.

Finished Block

Alternative Method for Placing Fabrics

Instead of using a light source to place succeeding fabric pieces, you can create an accurate placement for the next piece by trimming the previously sewn fabric(s) ¼" beyond the next line to be sewn.

1. Place a very thin ruler (even a postcard will do) along the line you will sew. Fold the lined side of the paper back on itself along the ruler. Remove the ruler.

2. Place the ¼" marking of the rotary ruler on the fold and trim the excess fabric along the ruler.

3. Place the next piece of fabric to be joined flush along this trimmed fabric edge, then sew as described previously.

You simply trim away the excess fabric before sewing the seam rather than after.

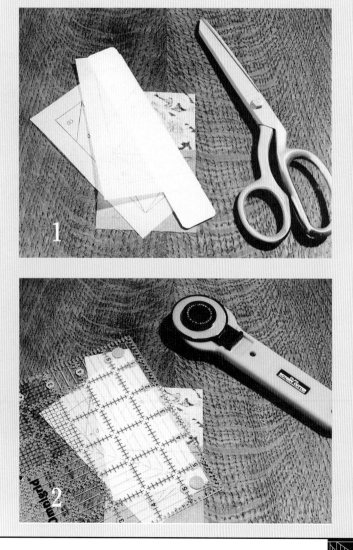

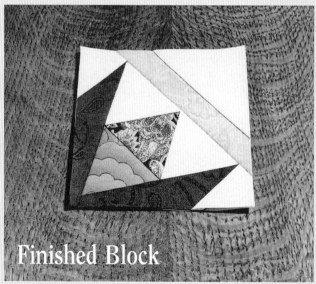

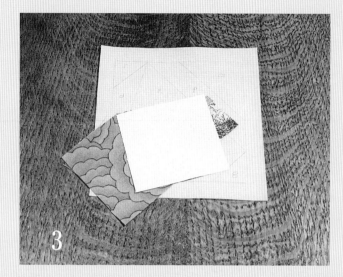

Finished Block

Sewing Tips

- Whenever possible, stitch in the direction of the points. This makes it easy to see that you are crossing the other line of stitching at the desired location.

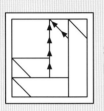

Stitch in the direction of points when possible.

- Use an open-toe presser foot on your machine for best visibility.
- If you have a knee-lift option on your sewing machine that controls the presser foot, use it. It not only leaves your hands free to hold the fabric in place, but it also drops the feed dogs, allowing the paper and fabric to slide easily under the presser foot.
- If you need several half-square triangles, cut oversize squares (finished short side of the triangle plus 1¼") and cut once diagonally.

Finished size: 1"
Cut one square 2¼" and cut once diagonally to yield two half-square triangles.

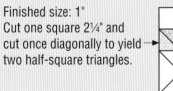

- If you need several quarter-square triangles, cut oversize squares (finished long side of the triangle plus 1½") and cut twice diagonally.

Finished size: 2"
Cut one square 3½" and cut twice diagonally to yield four quarter-square triangles.

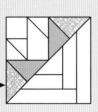

- When trimming seam allowances, fold the paper back slightly so it will not interfere.
- Use translucent tracing paper when you want to center a design on the first piece of fabric you place. The design is easier to see through the tracing paper.
- While sewing, hold the paper on both sides for better control.
- Finger-press each seam to quickly crease the pieces when your iron is not close at hand.
- Always overestimate the size of the pieces; you can trim away the excess. Remember, bigger is better!
- Since it is difficult to see from the reverse side if you are sewing striped or checked fabrics straight, you may want to choose fabrics that do not have directional designs.
- In areas where lots of seams come together, consider using a dark fabric to cover the seam allowances.
- If you open the fabric and the piece doesn't quite meet at a perfect point, simply take a deeper seam.
- Cut excess threads after sewing each seam.
- If the project calls for multiple blocks in identical fabrics, make one block to confirm your fabric choices. Make the remainder of the blocks in assembly-line fashion, adding the same piece to each block before adding the next piece.
- If you can't trim the seam allowances to ¼" wide because of cross-seam stitching, simply lift the seam to pull the stitching away from the paper.
- If the patchwork is tiny, use a smaller stitch length and smaller seam allowances.
- Consider using the wrong side of the fabric as the right side. Often, it appears as a lighter version of the print or as a solid.
- Iron delicate fabrics, such as lamés and silks, by pressing from the paper side after opening the piece. If you use copies from a photocopy machine, protect your iron from the ink, which may transfer onto a hot iron, with a scrap pressing cloth.
- Use Scotch™ Removable Magic™ tape to hold paper in place while tracing paper-piecing foundations or to repair a paper-piecing foundation. If necessary, press from the fabric side of the block with the tape in place, but take care not to touch the tape with your iron. Adjust the heat setting of the iron to "cotton" or a lower temperature. Pretest before you press. Caution: Press over removable tape only. Other tapes will tear the paper or even melt!

 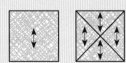

Making Two-Section Blocks

To make two-section blocks, piece the sections of the block as separate units. Trim joining seam allowances to ¼" and sew the two sections together to form the block. I find that it saves time to machine baste about an inch across any points that must meet exactly. Check to be sure that the designs will match before you actually join the two sections. Once you have pieced both sections, press the joining seam open (using a pressing cloth) to reduce bulk. Remove the paper in the seam allowance after joining the sections.

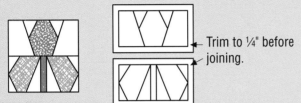

← Trim to ¼" before joining.

Two-section block

Sometimes it is possible to stitch two sections of a block together and then continue paper piecing across the joined sections. This option is appealing when you are using the same fabric in both areas and you want to eliminate the seam. Prior to joining the two sections of the block, trim the fabrics ¼" from the seam line that will be crossed. You can use this option for block P29 on page 50, the two little ducks. Piece each duck section, trim the fabric ¼" from the seam line, and join the two sections of the block. Sew #12 in one piece across the entire block, eliminating the middle seam in the upper section.

Add this piece after the two paper sections have been joined.

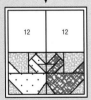

Add piece #18 to Snail block P31 in the same way. Piece the larger unit and trim the fabrics ¼" from the #18 line. Piece the smaller unit through #5 and trim the fabrics ¼" from the #18 line. Join the two units and sew piece #18 across the bottom.

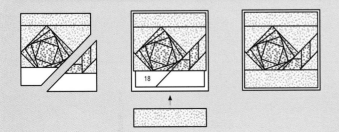

You can join the bottom or top halves of two or more blocks and then use the remaining joined foundation halves to add one piece of fabric across the joined blocks in the same way. I used this option to eliminate the center seam in the grass portion of block variations P46 and P47 in "Down on the Farm" on page 83.

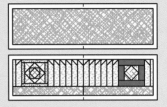

Making Pieced Units

Adding pieced units expands design possibilities. In the block designs, a pieced unit is noted by a "//" mark through the prepieced seam line, and the unit is assigned a number in the piecing sequence.

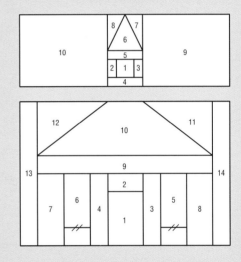

Single Straight-Seam Units

The Apartment House block, P42, and the Church block, P43, on page 57, both have single straight-seam, pieced units. To determine what size to cut and prepiece fabric pieces, measure the size of the rectangles and add ½" to ¾" for seam allowances. There is no need to cut them the exact size, because there is just one seam to match. Just cut them a little larger than the space they will fill. Sew the two rectangles together with the standard ¼"-wide seam allowance. Press the seam allowance to the darker side. Place this unit on the foundation with the seam along the indicated line on the paper. Stitch in place and trim any excess fabric after you have added the next piece (or use the alternative placement method described on page 12).

Tip: To keep the seams of pieced units from shifting when you add subsequent pieces of fabric, position the unit correctly. Machine baste it in place within the seam allowance just beyond the next cross seam. This keeps the seam in the proper position.

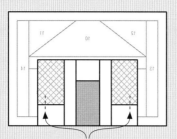

Machine baste to hold in place.

Double Straight-Seam Units

The Dog block, P34 on page 53, requires a pieced unit with two straight seams for #11. If you make only one block, cut the piece for the dog's nose the finished measurement plus an exact ½" for seam allowances. Cut two pieces of background fabric to the finished measurements plus ½" to ¾" for seam allowances. Sew the three pieces together with the nose fabric in the center. Stitch this to the block as one unit, aligning the seam lines with the drawing.

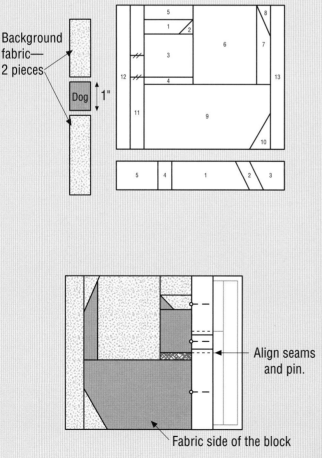

Background fabric— 2 pieces

Dog | 1"

Align seams and pin.

Fabric side of the block

When making several Dog blocks using the same fabrics, cut a strip from the dog-nose fabric the exact size (½" wide) plus ½" for seam allowances (1") and long enough to accommodate the number of pieced units needed. Cut strips from the background fabric the required size for the pieces above and below the dog nose, adding at least ½" for seams. Cut them long enough to accommodate the number of pieced units needed. Sew the dog-nose fabric strip between two background strips; then crosscut the strip set into 1"-wide units and attach them to the blocks.

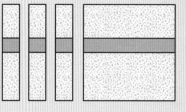

Using a Foundation to Create Pieced Units

When pieced units involve weird-angle pieces, units not easily measured with a ruler, or several bias seams, you can use a second foundation to prepiece these units. Trim the pieced unit ¼" from the adjoining seam, tear it away from this second foundation, and place it in position as a pieced unit. You can copy or trace the entire block or copy just that portion of the block that involves the pieced unit. If making multiples of the block, trace or photocopy one unit portion for each block.

You can also use the original foundation. Assemble the pieced unit on the foundation *before* you begin to paper piece the block. Once it is assembled, trim it ¼" from the adjoining seam. Carefully tear the unit away from the paper and put it aside. Repair the paper with removable tape. (See page 13 for more information on removable tape.) Piece the block in the usual manner, adding the pieced unit in the appropriate place.

The tail on Cow block P33 (piece #12) and the stem on Flower block F49 (piece #4) are examples of units that benefit from this option.

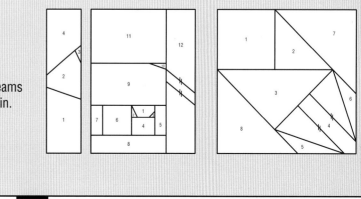

Block Designs

The designs are grouped into the following three categories:

Geometric Blocks	G31–G38
Flower Blocks	F24, F32–F71
Picture Blocks	P13, P28–P47

(F24 and P13 are repeated from *Easy Reversible Vests*.)

I introduced these block categories and the numbering sequences in *Easy Machine Paper Piecing* and continued them in *Easy Reversible Vests* and *Easy Paper-Pieced Keepsake Quilts*. You can use all the patterns presented here with the blocks in those books, expanding the design possibilities even further.

Block Photos

The block photos only suggest possibilities for fabric placement. There are many other options that will yield different patchwork variations from the same line drawing.

4" Block Designs

You can trace, photocopy, enlarge, or reduce the piecing foundations to create quilt blocks. The lines on the block design represent the sewing lines, and the numbers represent the piecing sequence. Paper piecing blocks is quick; however, a block with nine pieces takes half as much time to sew as a block with eighteen pieces. A block that has more or tinier pieces is no more difficult to sew than a block with a few large pieces. It only takes more stitching time.

The 4" block design represents the wrong side of the block. This is of no consequence for symmetrical blocks. However, asymmetrical blocks result in the reverse pattern on the finished side.

Piecing foundations that have several merging seams at one corner are shown with an optional seam variation indicated with a dotted line. See page 60 for more information about added seam variations.

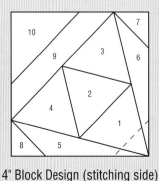

4" Block Design (stitching side)

Block-Front Drawings

These small drawings show how the finished blocks will appear from the fabric side. Blocks with a diagonal focus are presented in a four-block rotation so that a design resulting from this placement is evident. Rotating the blocks in other ways will result in different designs. Several two-section blocks offer other combination options, and some of these are depicted in the block-front drawings. You may photocopy the block-front drawings and use them with the quilt-layout worksheets described on page 63 to create your own quilt plans. Arrange the blocks in several settings and in conjunction with other blocks or fabric squares and borders until you have created a pleasing design. When you are satisfied, photocopy the design layout several times and use colored pencils to try out different color schemes. Always use the block-front drawings to make your design and color selection, and note your choices on the unmarked side of the corresponding 4" piecing foundations.

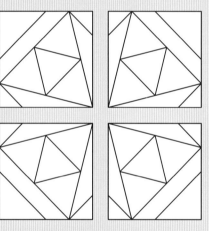

Block-Front Drawings

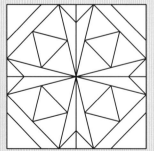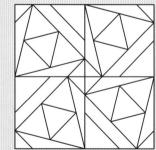

Different block rotations result in different design options.

Geometric, Flower, and Picture Blocks

G31
(page 25)

G32
(page 26)

G33
(page 26)

G34
(page 26)

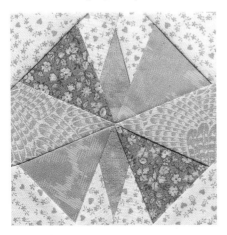

G35
(page 27)

G36
(page 27)

G37
(page 28)

G38
(page 28)

F32
(page 29)

F33
(page 30)

F34
(page 30)

F35
(page 31)

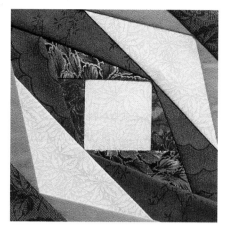

F36
(page 31)

F37
(page 32)

F38
(page 32)

F39
(page 33)

F40
(page 33)

F41
(page 34)

F42
(page 34)

F43
(page 35)

F44
(page 35)

F45
(page 36)

F46
(page 36)

F47
(page 37)

F48
(page 37)

F49
(page 38)

F50
(page 38)

F51
(page 39)

F52
(page 39)

F53
(page 40)

F54
(page 40)

F55
(page 41)

F56
(page 41)

F57
(page 42)

F58
(page 42)

F59
(page 43)

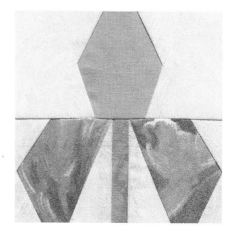

F60
(page 43)

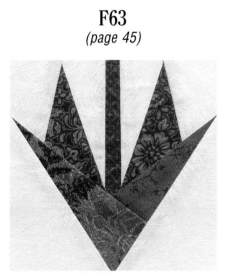

F61
(page 44)

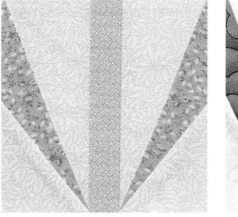

F62
(page 44)

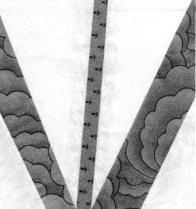

F63
(page 45)

F64
(page 45)

F65
(page 46)

F66
(page 46)

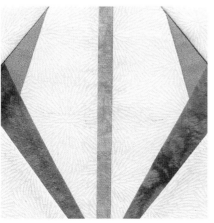

F24
(page 29)

F67
(page 47)

F68
(page 47)

F69
(page 48)

F70
(page 48)

F71
(page 49)

P13
(page 49)

P28
(page 50)

P29
(page 50)

P30
(page 51)

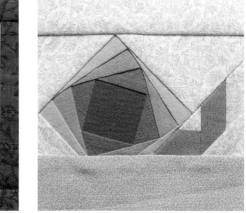

P31
(page 51)

P32
(page 52)

P33
(page 52)

P34
(page 53)

P35
(page 53)

P36
(page 54)

P37
(page 54)

P38
(page 55)

P39
(page 55)

P40
(page 56)

P41
(page 56)

P42
(page 57)

P43
(page 57)

P44
(page 58)

P45
(page 58)

P46
(page 59)

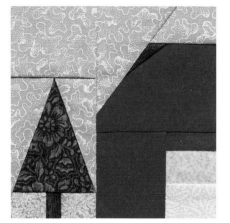
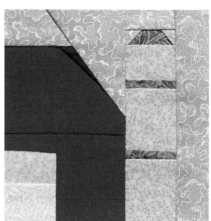
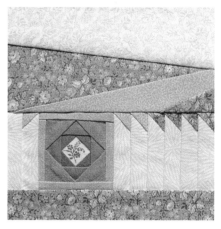

P47
(page 59)

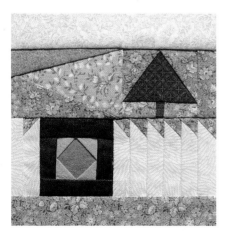

Geometric Blocks

G31
Color photo: page 17

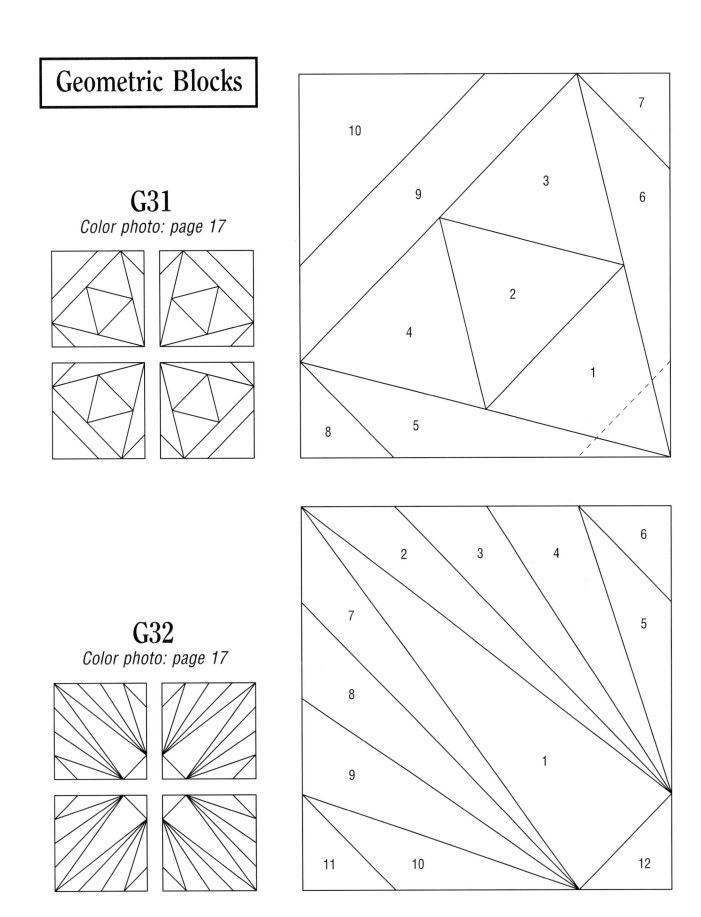

G32
Color photo: page 17

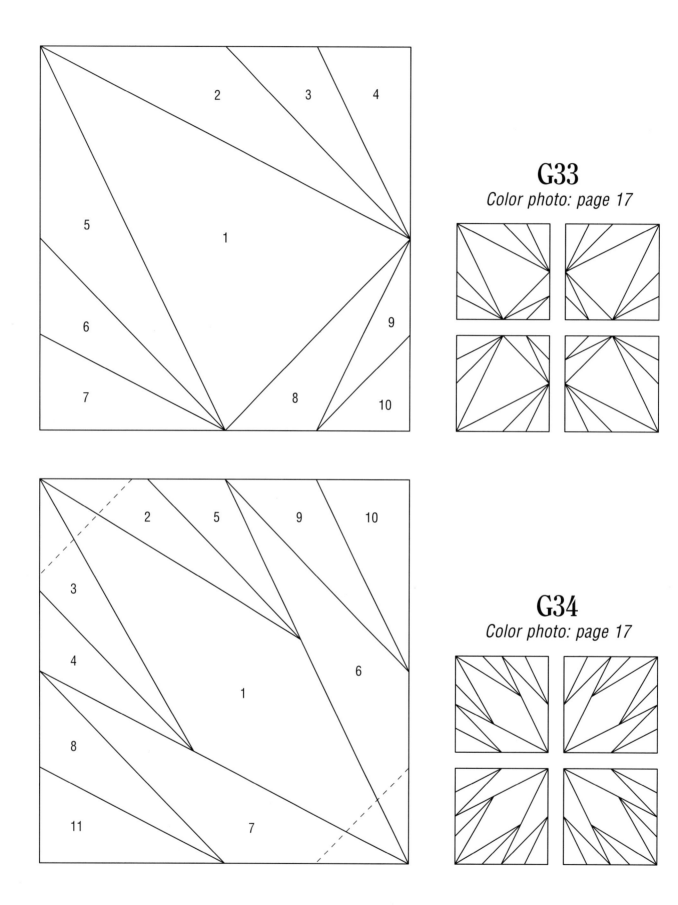

G33

Color photo: page 17

G34

Color photo: page 17

G35

Color photo: page 17

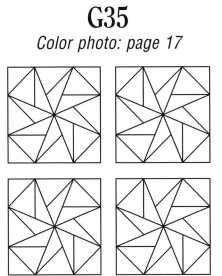

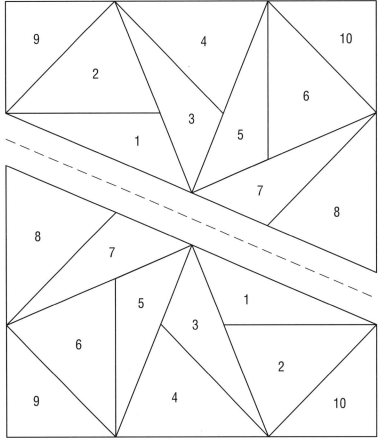

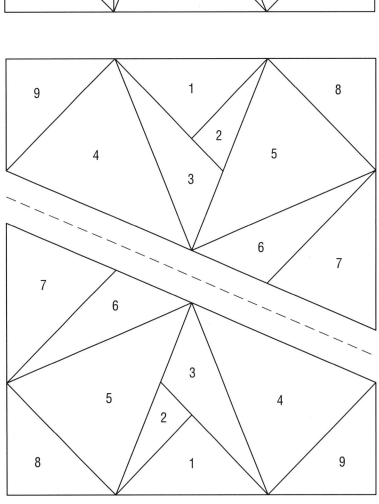

G36

Color photo: page 17

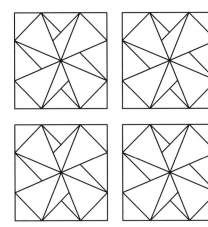

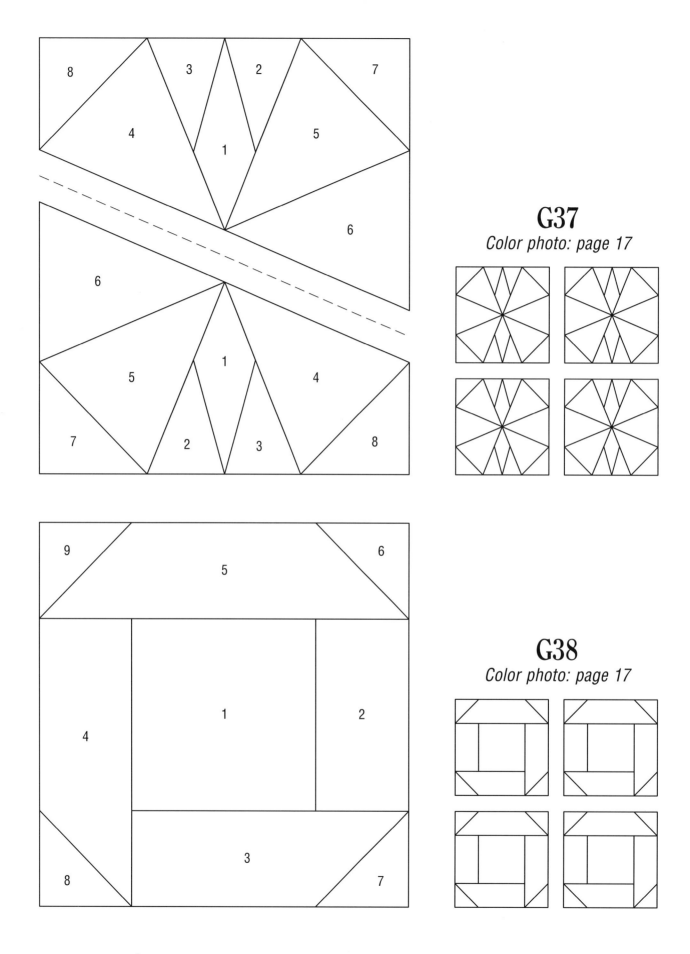

G37

Color photo: page 17

G38

Color photo: page 17

Flower Blocks

F24
Color photo: page 21

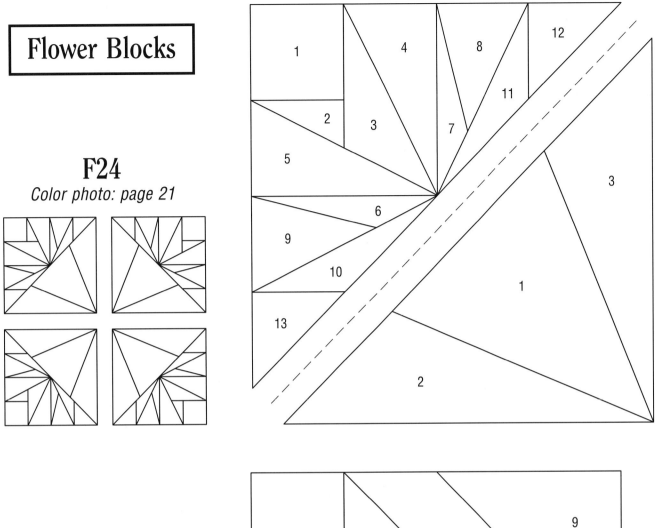

F32
Color photo: page 17

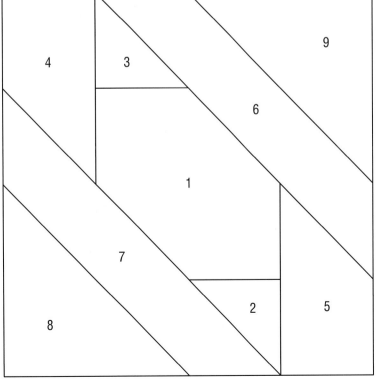

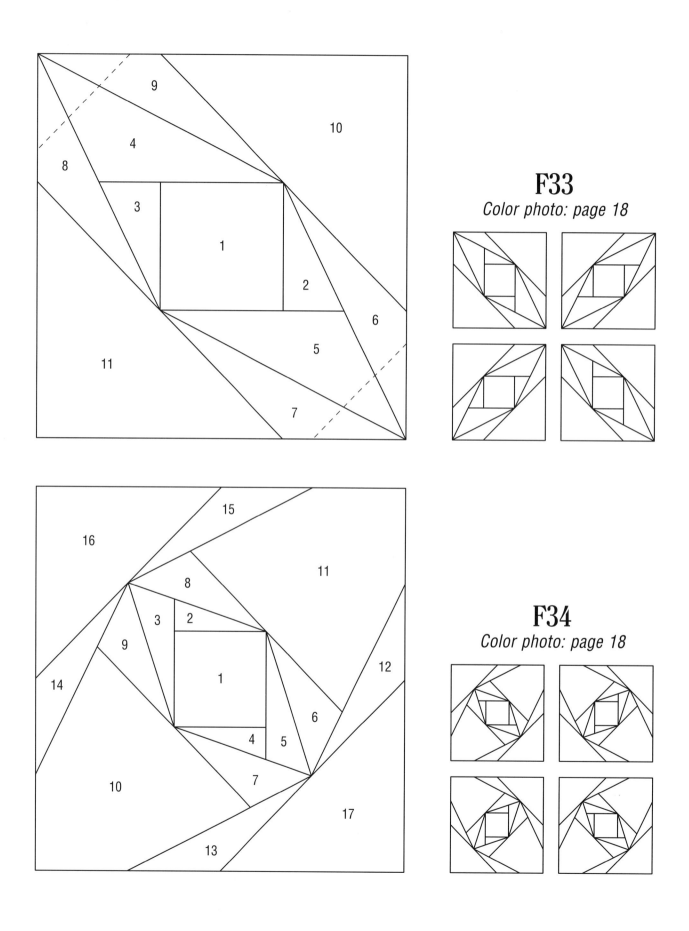

F33
Color photo: page 18

F34
Color photo: page 18

F35

Color photo: page 18

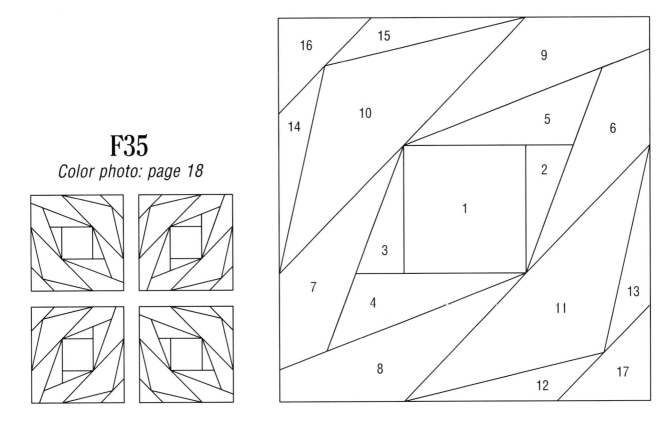

F36

Color photo: page 18

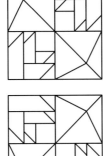

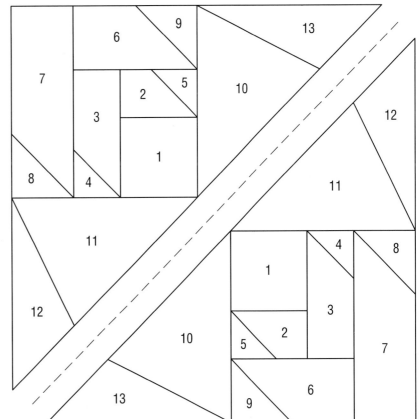

 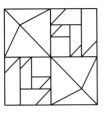

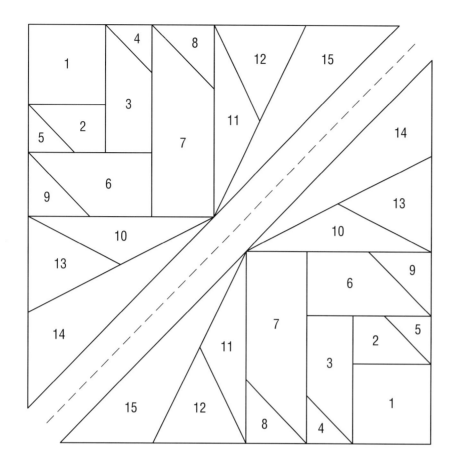

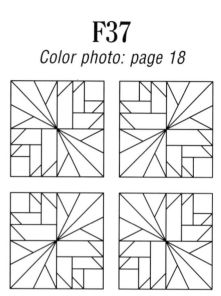

F37
Color photo: page 18

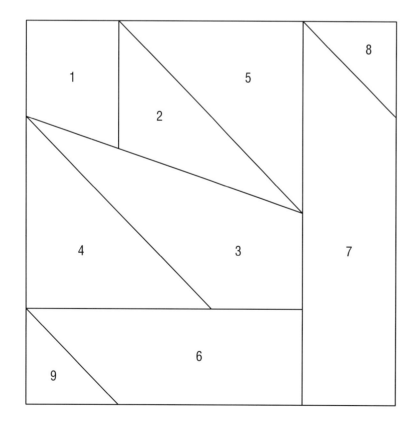

F38
Color photo: page 18

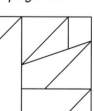
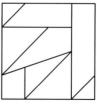

F39

Color photo: page 18

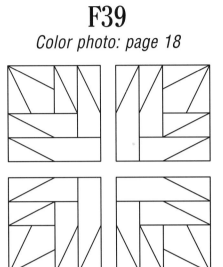

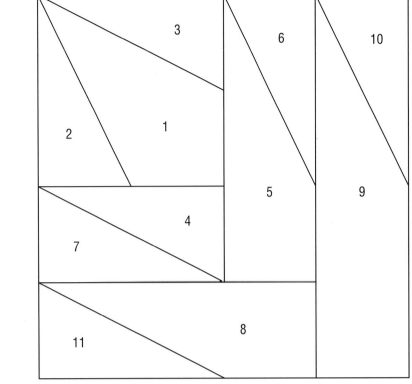

F40

Color photo: page 18

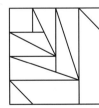
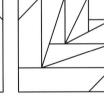
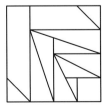

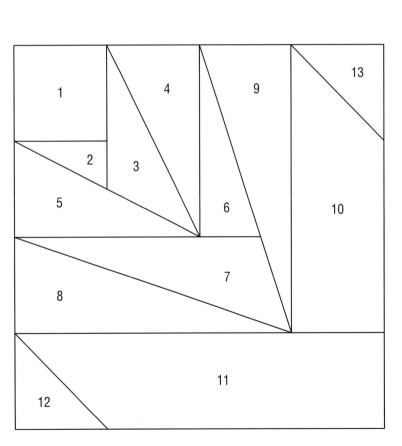

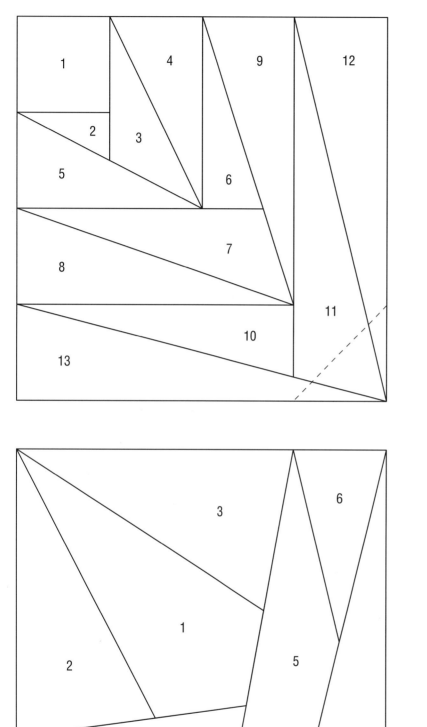

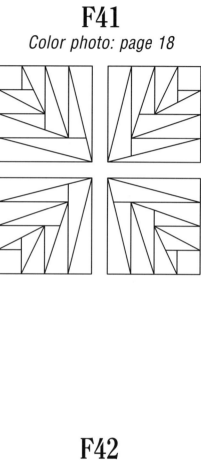

F41

Color photo: page 18

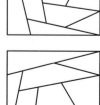

F42

Color photo: page 19

F43

Color photo: page 19

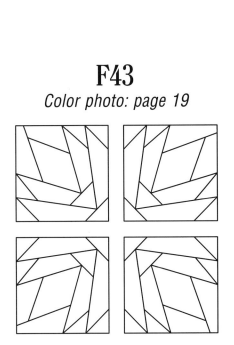

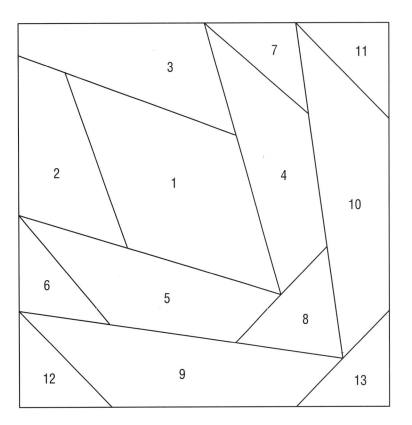

F44

Color photo: page 19

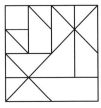

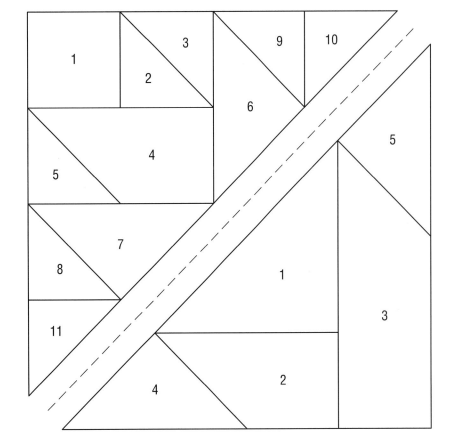

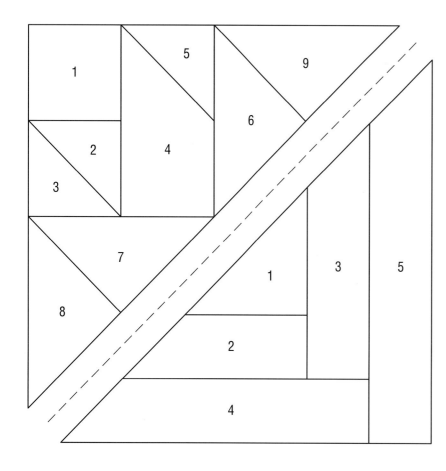

F45

Color photo: page 19

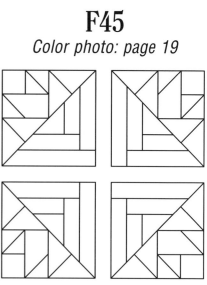

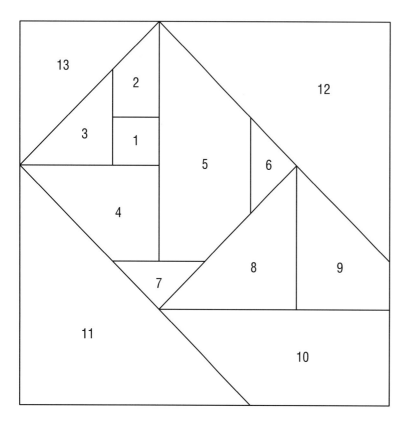

F46

Color photo: page 19

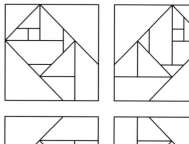

F47

Color photo: page 19

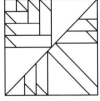

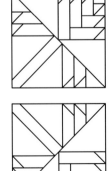

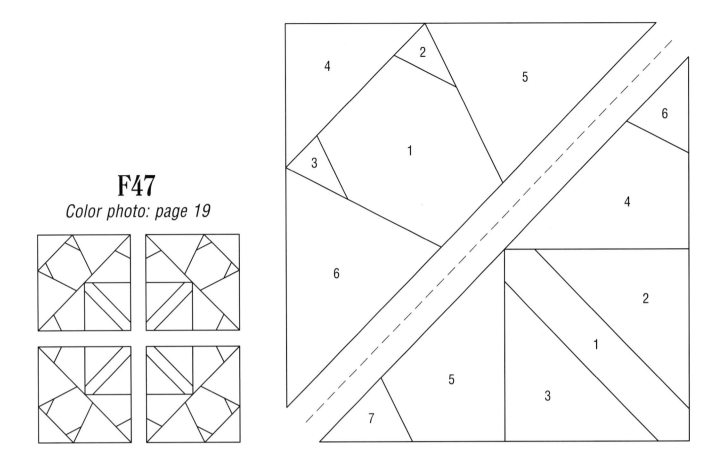

F48

Color photo: page 19

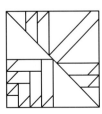

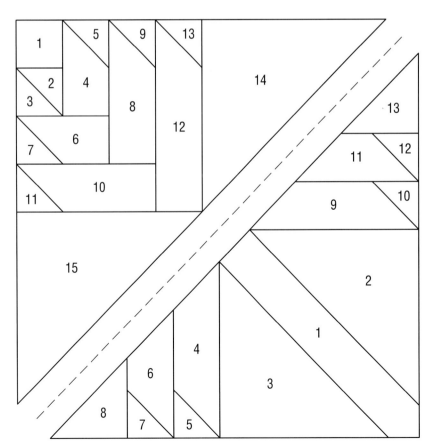

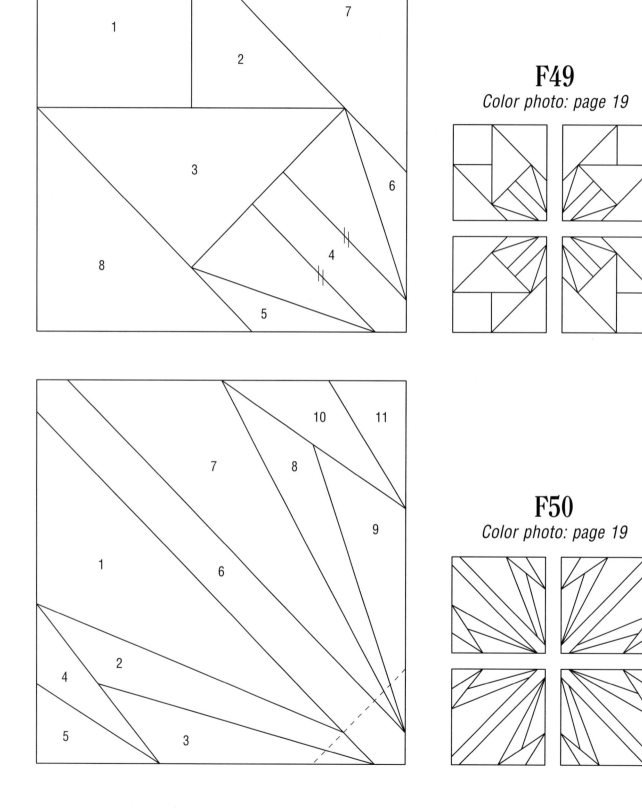

F49
Color photo: page 19

F50
Color photo: page 19

F51

Color photo: page 20

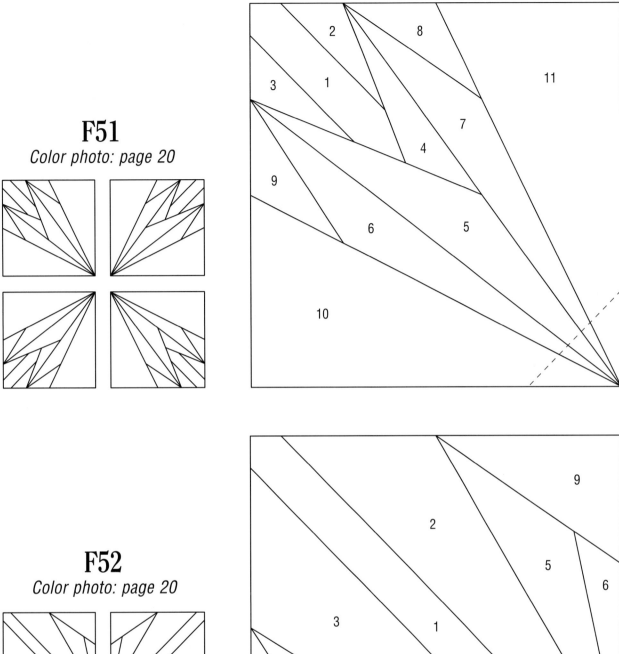

F52

Color photo: page 20

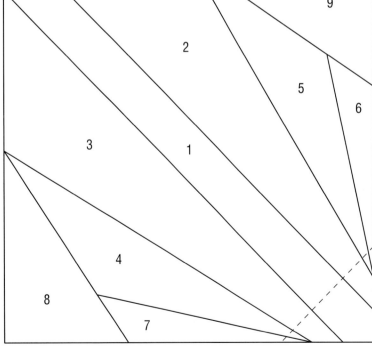

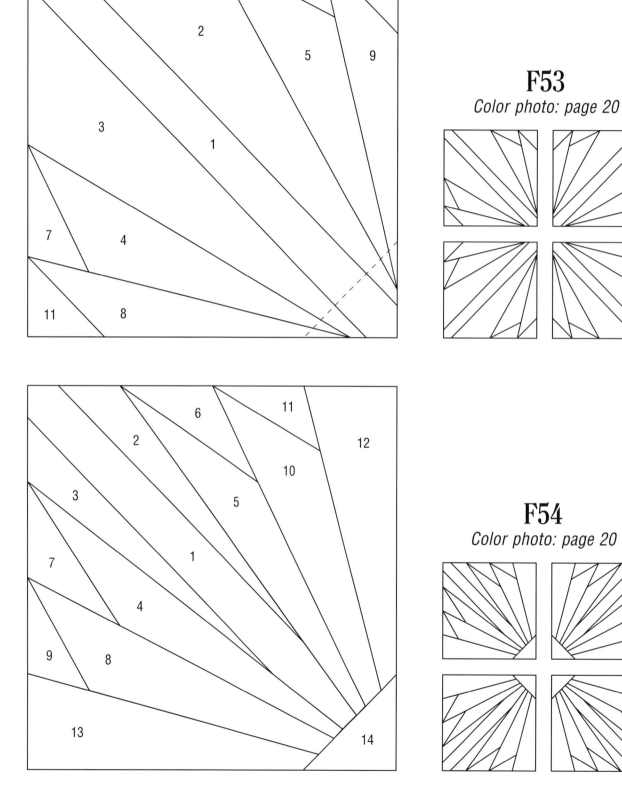

F53

Color photo: page 20

F54

Color photo: page 20

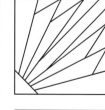

Quilt Blocks

F55

Color photo: page 20

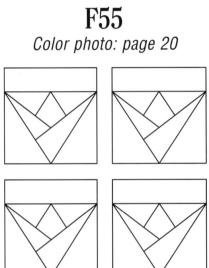

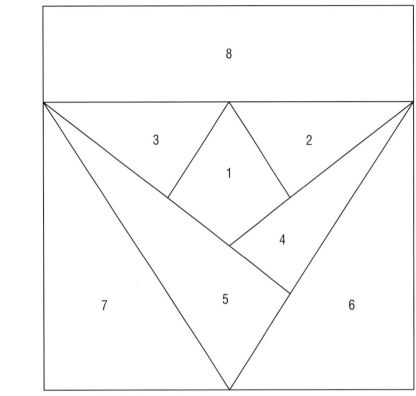

F56

Color photo: page 20

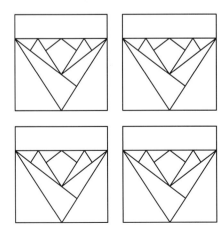

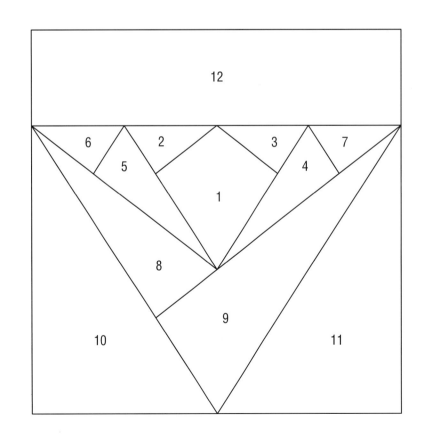

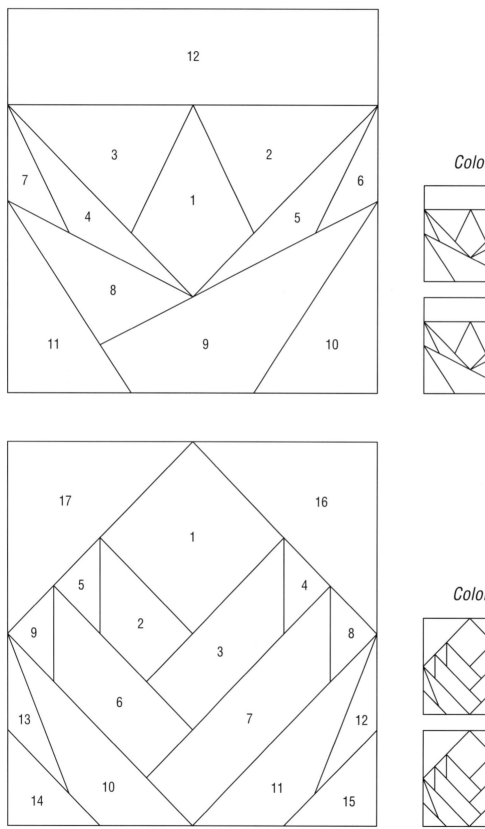

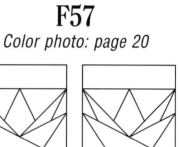

F57
Color photo: page 20

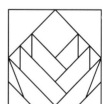

F58
Color photo: page 20

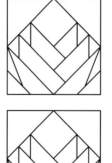

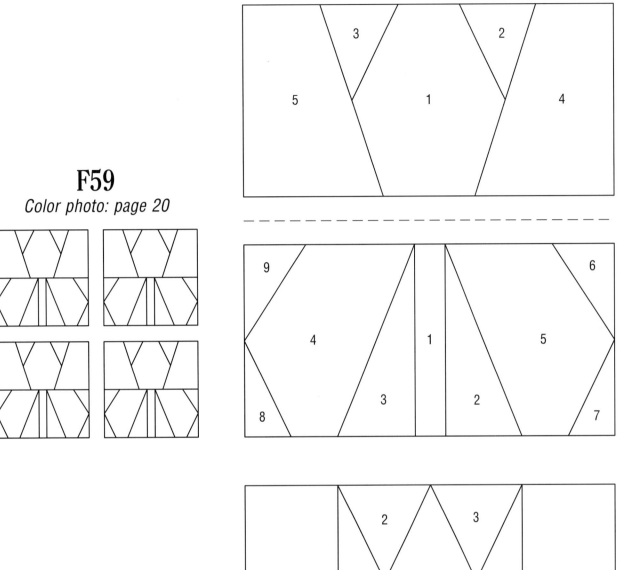

F59

Color photo: page 20

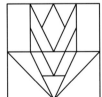

F60

Color photo: page 21

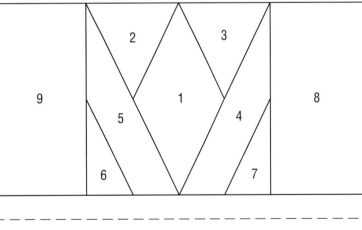
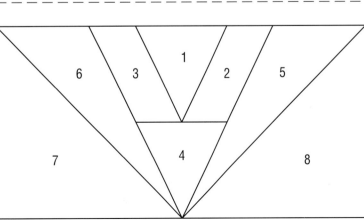
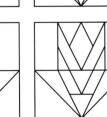

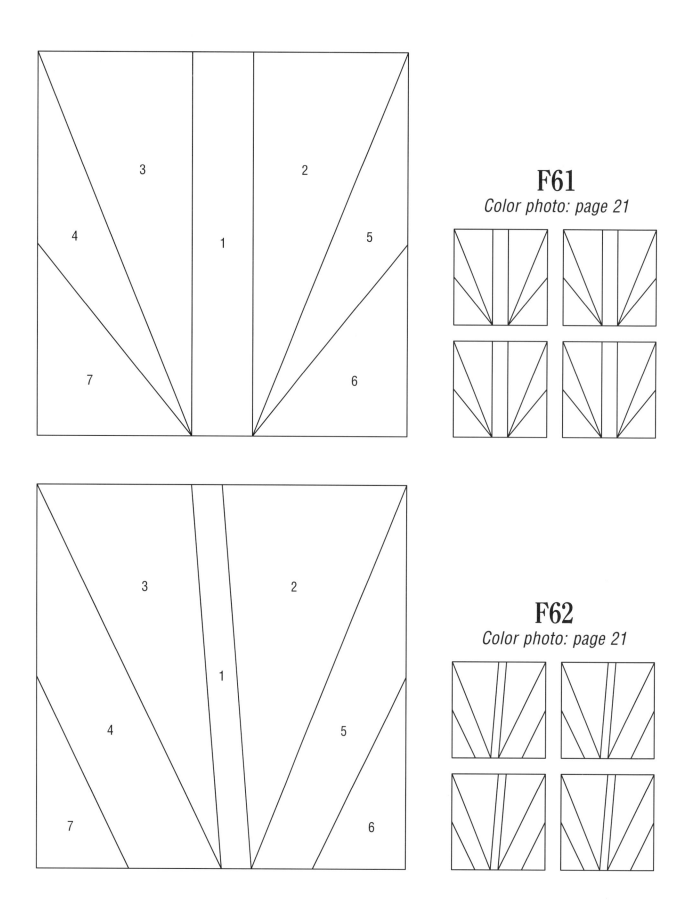

F61
Color photo: page 21

F62
Color photo: page 21

F63

Color photo: page 21

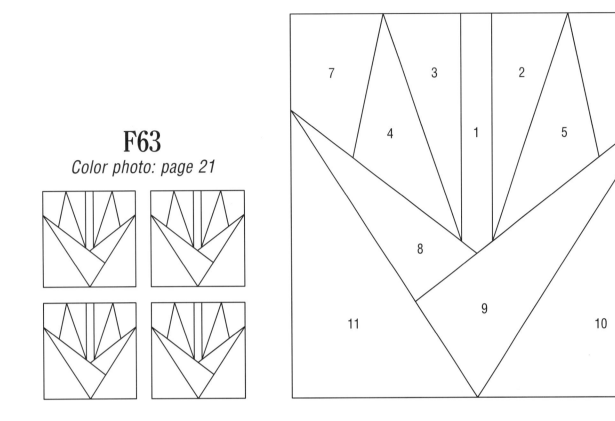

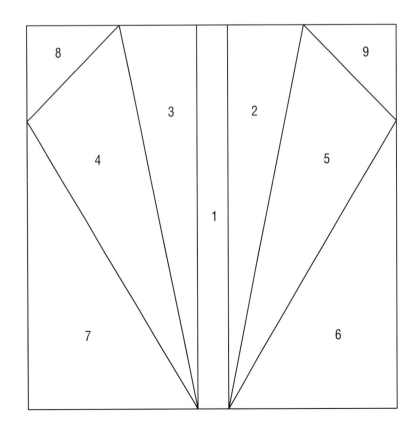

F64

Color photo: page 21

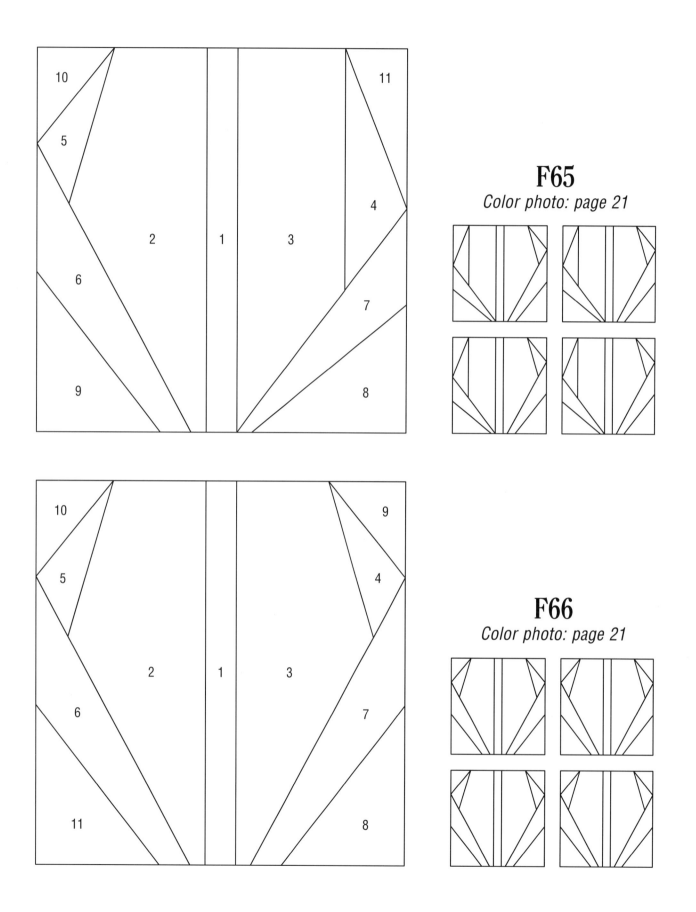

F65

Color photo: page 21

F66

Color photo: page 21

F67

Color photo: page 21

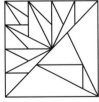

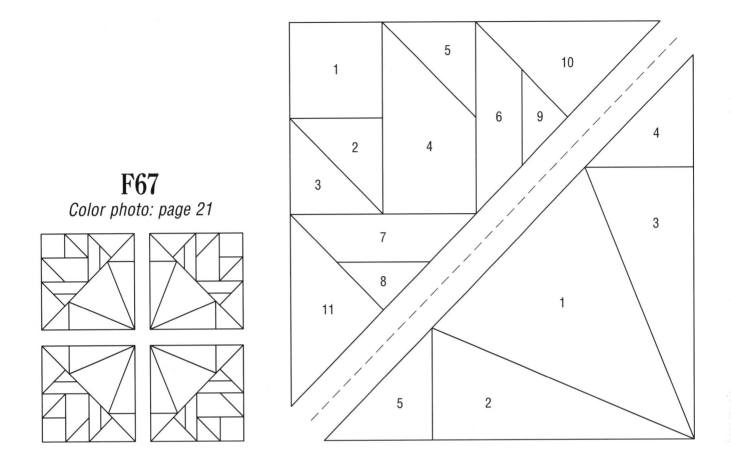

F68

Color photo: page 22

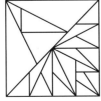

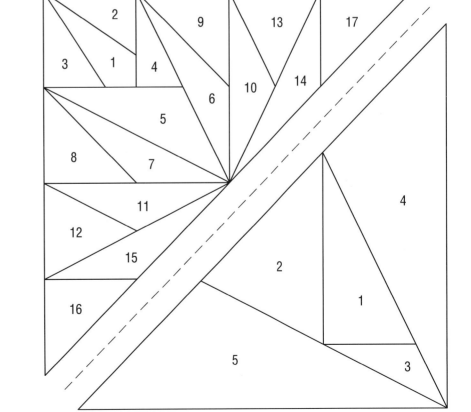

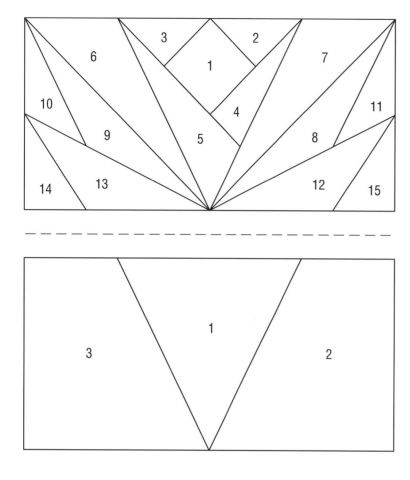

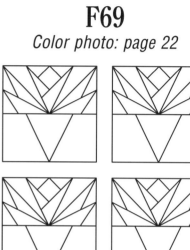

F69

Color photo: page 22

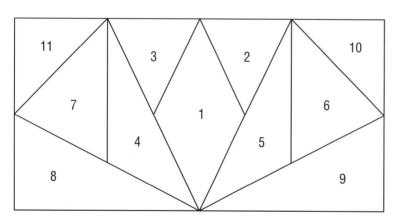

F70

Color photo: page 22

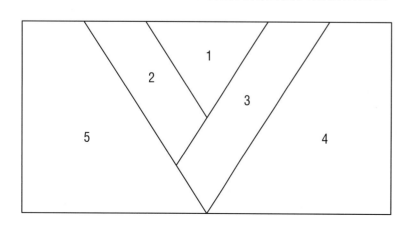

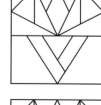

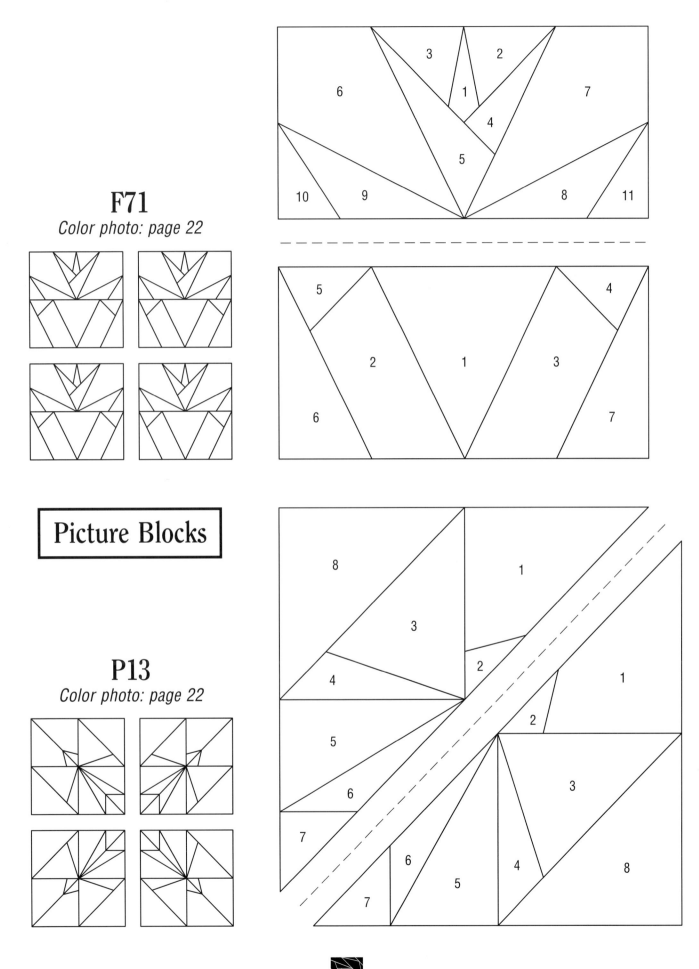

F71

Color photo: page 22

Picture Blocks

P13

Color photo: page 22

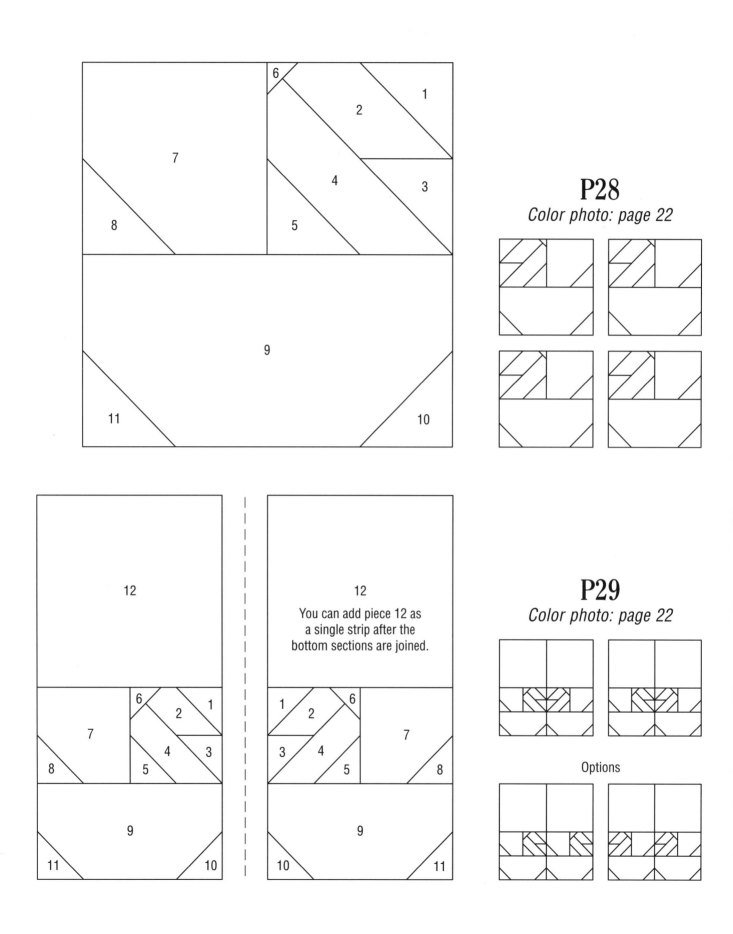

P28
Color photo: page 22

P29
Color photo: page 22

You can add piece 12 as
a single strip after the
bottom sections are joined.

Options

P30

Color photo: page 22

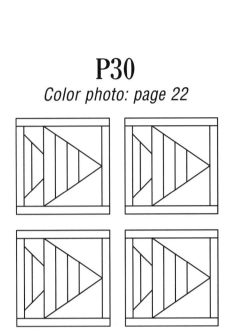

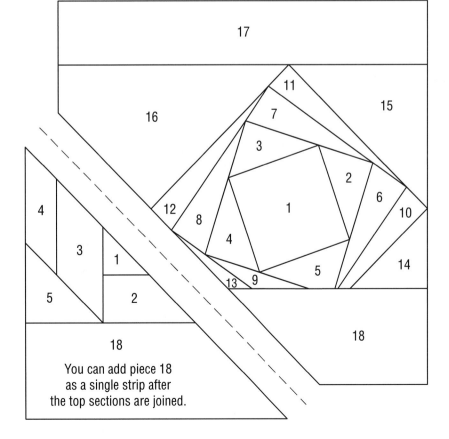

P31

Color photo: page 22

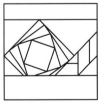
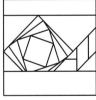
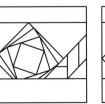
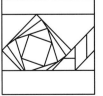

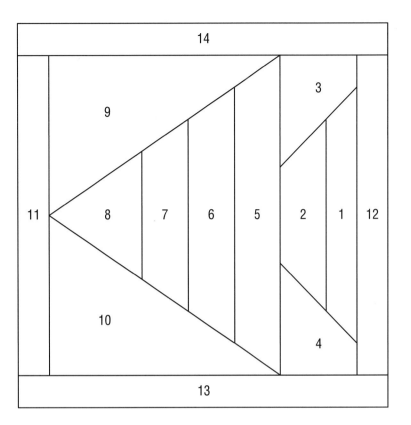

You can add piece 18
as a single strip after
the top sections are joined.

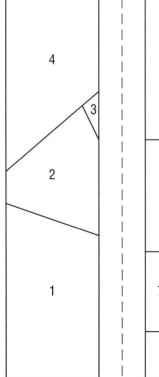

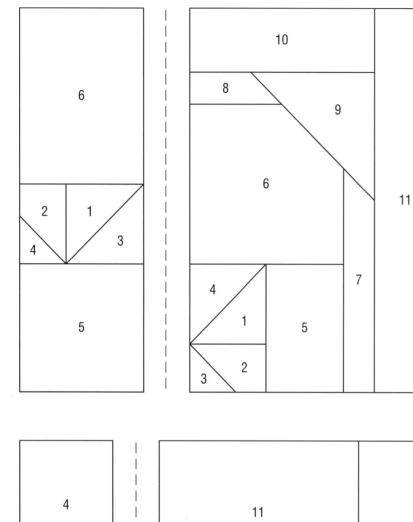

P32

Color photo: page 23

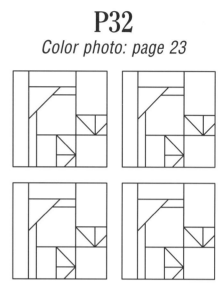

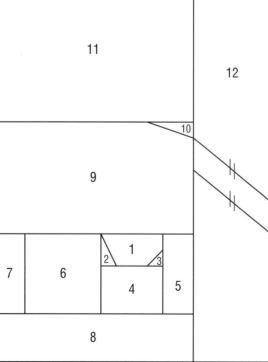

P33

Color photo: page 23

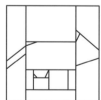

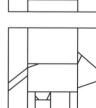

P34

Color photo: page 23

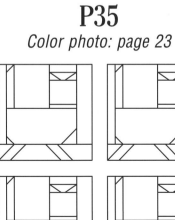

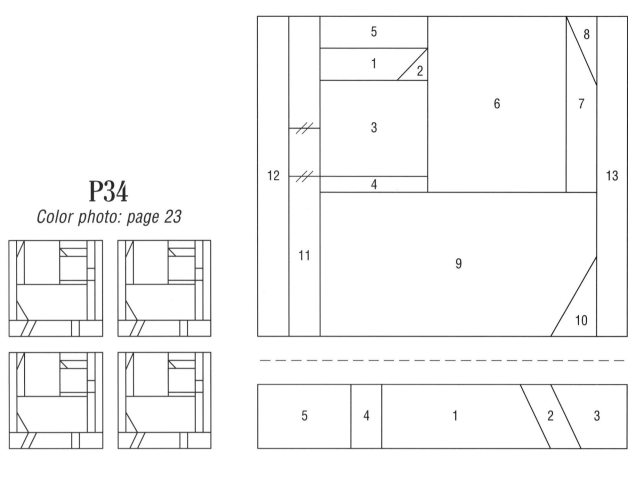

P35

Color photo: page 23

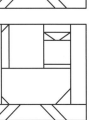

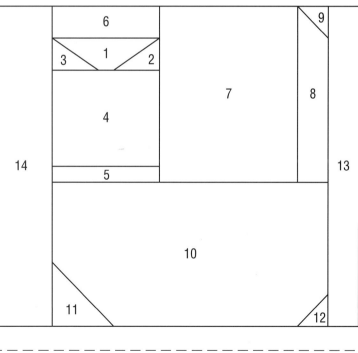

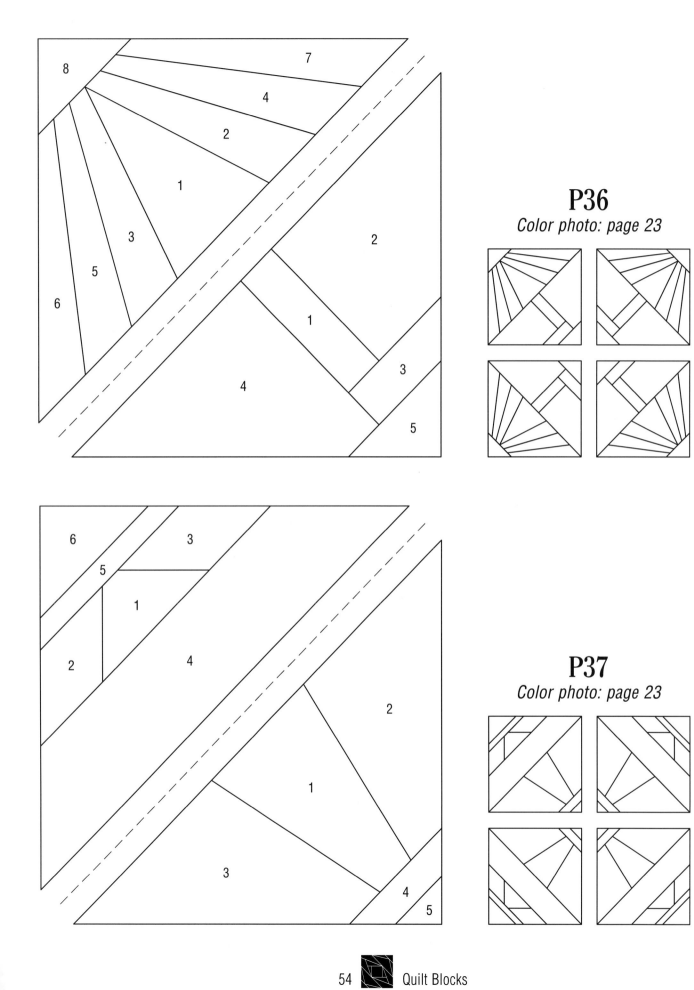

P36
Color photo: page 23

P37
Color photo: page 23

P38

Color photo: page 23

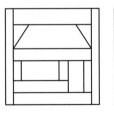
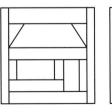
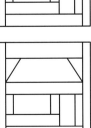

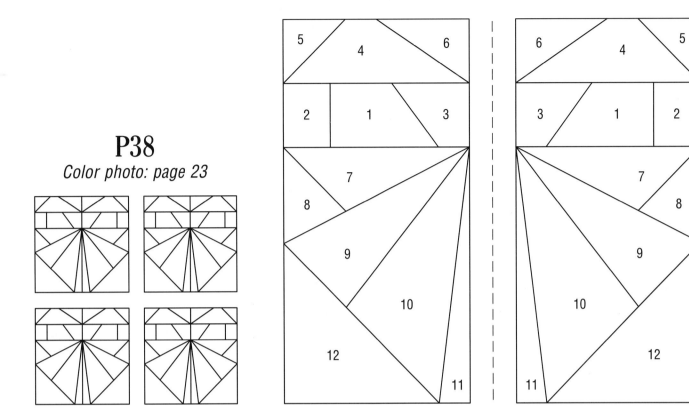

P39

Color photo: page 23

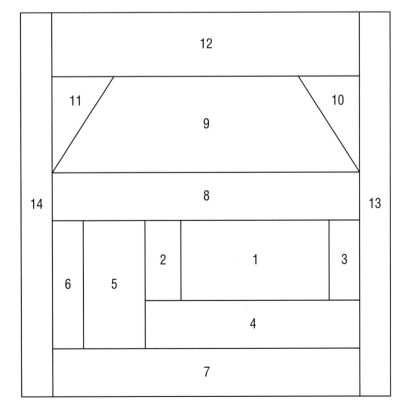

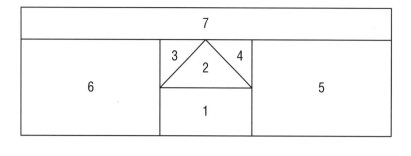

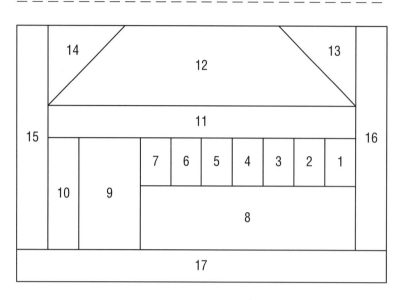

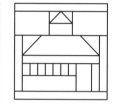

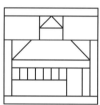

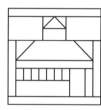

P40

Color photo: page 23

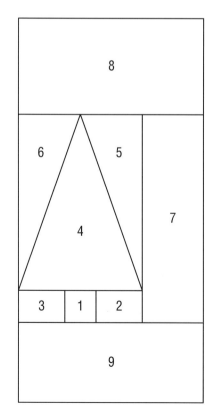

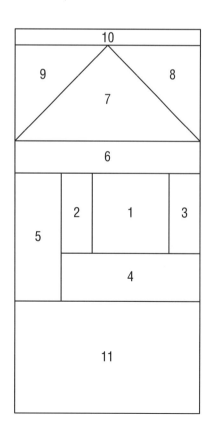

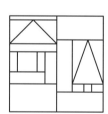

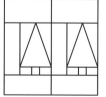

P41

Color photo: page 24

Option

Options

P42

Color photo: page 24

Option

Options

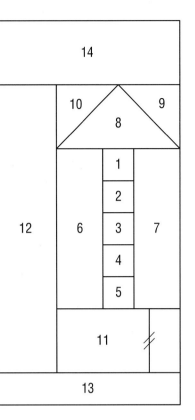

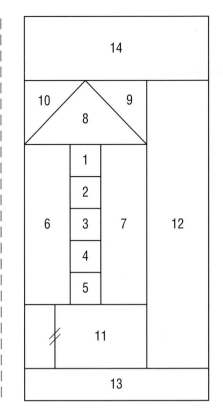

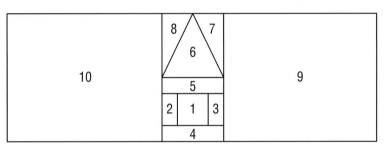

P43

Color photo: page 24

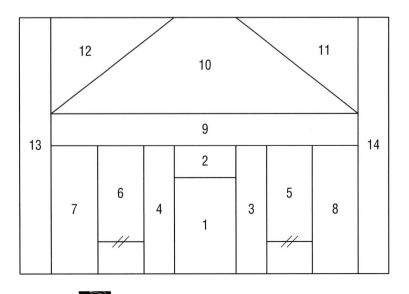

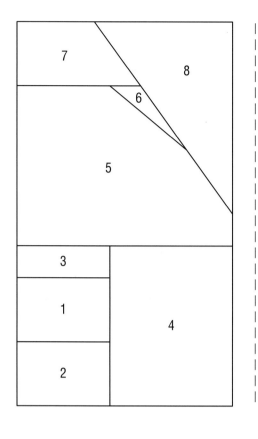

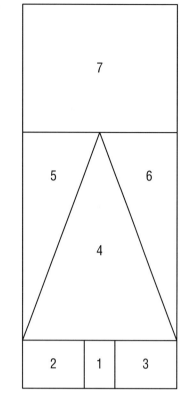

P44

Color photo: page 24

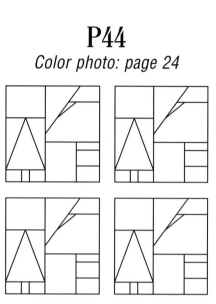

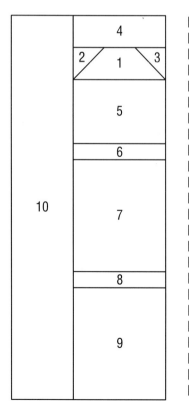

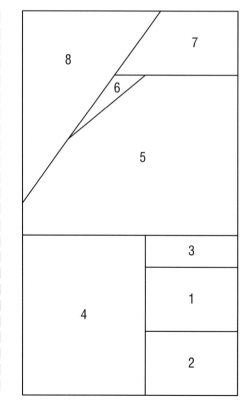

P45

Color photo: page 24

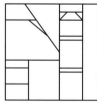

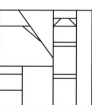

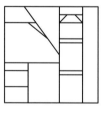

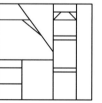

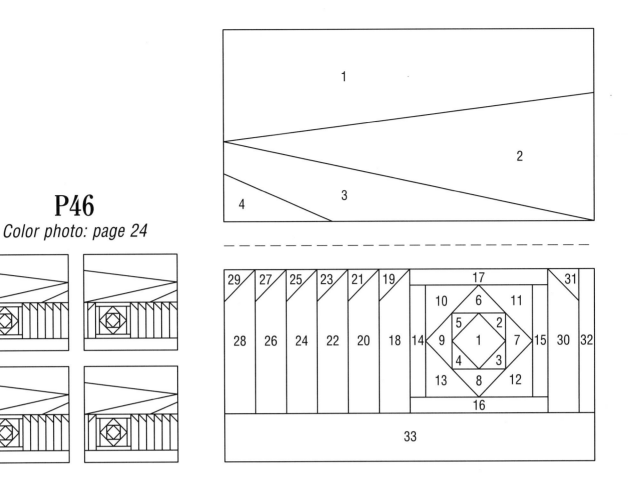

P46

Color photo: page 24

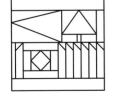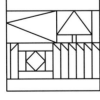

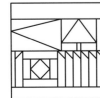

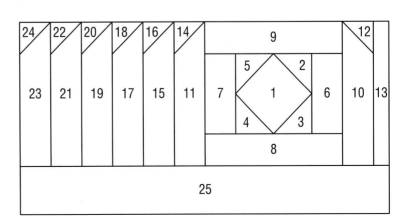

P47

Color photo: page 24

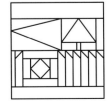

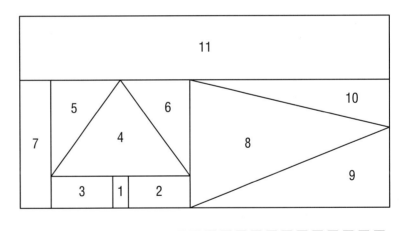

Block and Quilt Design Possibilities

The block designs presented in this book represent only a fraction of the possible variations. Experiment with the following methods to change the look of the blocks or simplify construction.

Eliminating and Adding Seam Lines

You can sew the block designs as they are presented or create variations by eliminating one or more seam lines. You will not receive demerits if you don't piece all the sections of the blocks as they appear. You can eliminate any line if you can continue the piecing sequence with no consequence. The elimination of seam lines not only creates a new design, but also simplifies the block so that it is quicker to piece. The illustration below shows how to make variations of the same block by eliminating seam lines.

You can also add seam lines to create block-design variations if the piecing sequence continues across the added lines or if the added seam is the last seam. Additional seam lines can make a design more intricate or they can actually simplify a block.

Eliminate merging seams in the corner of a block by adding a seam across the corner. This is a helpful option if you plan to piece two or four blocks in rotation. Measure the same distance from the corner along both sides and connect the points. The merging corner seams are no more! Block designs that benefit from an addi-

tional seam across the corner have a dotted line to indicate the last seam variation.

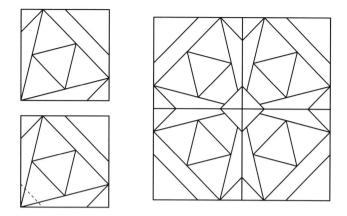

Exploring Value Options

Changing the value of the fabric in certain areas of the block further increases design possibilities. Value is the relative amount of lightness or darkness in colors. A black-and-white photograph shows only values. Just one block pattern offers a variety of design possibilities—simply change the value placement to change the design. Experiment by coloring sections of the block-front drawings with a pencil using light, medium, and dark shadings. You may discover several design options. Once you choose the values, use colored pencils to experiment with color in the design. The block below looks very different with different value placements.

Making Fabric Choices

There are so many fabric possibilities. Use a group of coordinated fabrics to complete a project of only one block design or a combination of several block designs. Or, select one fabric to set the theme or tone of your quilt and choose others that coordinate with this fabric. Use fabrics resembling grass, sky, or trees to make scenic block designs look realistic.

Incorporate novelty fabrics, such as silk and lamé, into designs. Since the paper helps to stabilize the fabric and you sew with short stitches, you can use fabrics you might normally avoid when doing patchwork.

Explore the use of fabric motifs. If you use tracing paper for the block foundations, you can center specific elements printed on the fabric in the #1 position to create a special look.

For an interesting and varied quilt, use a simple block design with a variety of scraps. With a ready supply of paper patterns and a scrap basket next to your sewing machine, you have the opportunity to sew blocks when short spurts of time are available. It is amazing how quickly the blocks accumulate when you use this approach.

Combining Blocks

Many of the block designs presented combine well with other blocks or parts of blocks. Explore several ways to "mix and match" the following designs. I hope you will be delighted with the new patterns you discover!

Blocks with Diagonal Designs

Several block designs have diagonal lines that radiate from one corner. Four blocks placed together and rotated allow new designs to emerge from the combination. The flowers in "Garden Weave" on page 81 were created in this way.

Sometimes four blocks placed in rotation result in a pleasant surprise. Four Butterfly blocks (P13 on page 22) placed this way produce a star pattern. "The Aquatic Community" on page 83 contains Butterfly blocks used in this manner.

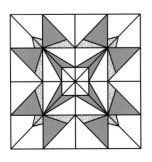

When the diagonal design continues through the block from corner to corner, the potential for creating secondary designs exists. "Southern Cross" on page 82, "Unchained Melody" on page 82, "Wedding Flower Rings" on page 87, "Poinsettia Galaxy" on page 86, and "Night Blooms" on page 85 all have blocks with diagonal focuses that create secondary designs.

Use different values to highlight these secondary designs. In the following example, the value in some portions of the blocks was changed to accentuate the secondary design that formed.

Kaleidoscope Block Designs

The kaleidoscope pattern is the basis for block designs G35–G37. You can create patchwork with subtle circular shapes by using different values in different sections of the block. Place a group of identical or different kaleidoscope patterns together and shade in various sections with different values to explore the design possibilities.

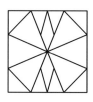 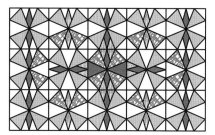

Create delightful circular shapes
with Kaleidoscope block designs.

Scenic Block Designs

The block designs that depict scenes (P39–P47) combine in a variety of ways to create patchwork pictures. "Down on the Farm" on page 83 and "Town and Country" on page 84 are examples of this option.

Two-Section Blocks

You can alter the piecing of some two-section blocks to form new designs. Make the little ducks in block P29 as presented, or make two ducks and join them as shown below. You can also piece the House-and-Tree block, P41, and the Apartment House block, P42, in different combinations.

Original design   Options

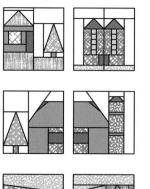

The units of some two-section blocks are interchangeable, such as the top and bottom halves of the blocks above right. Combine different tops and bottoms

or combine two tops or two bottoms for even more design options.

The above top and bottom sections are interchangeable. The designs below are created by the top and bottom sections.

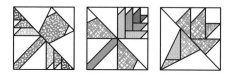

Two top or bottom sections of
the same block can also be combined.

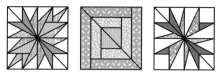

You can also interchange the following two-section Picture blocks as shown.

Original designs   New combinations

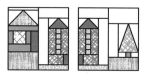

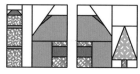

Design Combinations

Some of the blocks can be combined with other blocks to form two-part designs. Use any diagonal Flower blocks F38–F49 with any diagonal Leaf blocks F50–F54. Some of the flower tops have stems and some do not. When you use these blocks in a quilt, the corners of the alternating plain squares do not continue the stem portion. I considered creating a block that continued the stem portion, but it seemed unnecessary as the block combinations gave the illusion of continuity. In the Iris Medallion quilt on page 87, the Iris block and a diagonal Leaf block create a striking new design.

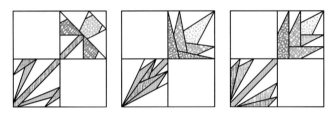

Two-part diagonal flower block combinations

Combine vertical Flower blocks F55–F60 with vertical Leaf blocks F61–F66 to create new designs. "How Does Your Garden Grow?" on page 88 illustrates several of these combinations. All the stems in blocks F63–F66 are the same width and match the stem in Iris block F59. The stem in F61 is wider and the stem in F62 is slightly askew and does not match the stem in the Iris block. The illustrations below show some of the mix-and-match options.

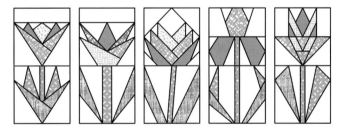

Two-part vertical flower block combinations

Combine the two halves of the Barn blocks (P44 and P45) to create the entire barn. You can also create a longer fence and larger landscape by joining the two blocks containing the picket fences displaying quilts, P46 and P47.

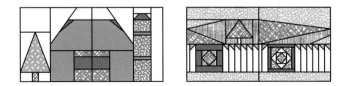

Quilt Layouts

To create original quilt designs, make a quilt layout work sheet to arrange the block-front drawings in different combinations, positions, and color schemes. On graph paper, draw a grid of 1" squares in a straight set or in a diagonal set, in the size you intend to make. Each square represents one block. Photocopy the grid layout for a ready supply of work sheets.

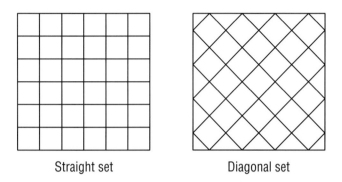

Straight set   Diagonal set

Select a group of blocks and cut out photocopies of the block-front drawings. If you are going to combine sections, cut the sections apart. Move the blocks around on the layout work sheet in different positions and rotations until you achieve a pleasing design. Consider using some plain fabric squares between the patchwork blocks. Try using borders and lattice strips to separate the blocks. Experiment with different combinations to see how the elements interact.

Try looking at the "Gallery of Quilts" on pages 81–88 to find a block setting you like. You can use one of the layouts shown with different block designs.

The blocks do not all have to be the same size. If you use 6" blocks, it's easy to use 3" blocks in the same quilt. You can add 1"-wide borders to 4" blocks to create 6" blocks or you can enlarge 4" block designs to 6" with a photocopy machine. Combine four 6" blocks to create a single 12" square and add lattices for a full-size quilt.

Project Size

To determine the size of a straight-set quilt layout, multiply the number of blocks vertically and horizontally by the size of the block. For example, a quilt with twenty-four blocks, each 4" square, set four blocks by six blocks, measures 16" x 24" without borders. The same quilt made with 6" blocks measures 24" x 36" without borders.

For diagonally set quilt layouts, multiply the size of the block by 1.4142 to arrive at the diagonal measurement of the block. For example, a 4" block has a diagonal measurement of 5⅝". Multiply this number by the number of blocks vertically and horizontally in the quilt to determine the quilt size without borders.

Use half-square triangles (with the straight of grain on the short sides) for corner triangles. Determine the finished size of the short edge of the triangle; add ⅞" to this figure and cut a square that size. Then cut it once diagonally to yield two corner triangles.

Use quarter-square triangles (with the straight of grain on the long side) for side triangles. Determine the finished size of the long side of the triangle; add 1¼" and cut a square that size. Then cut it twice diagonally to yield four side setting triangles.

The following chart indicates the finished diagonal measurement of a variety of finished block sizes and the square sizes to cut for the corner and side triangles.

Finished Block Size	Diagonal Size	Corner Triangles	Side Triangles
3"	4¼"	3"	5½"
4"	5⅝"	3¾"	6⅞"
5"	7⅛"	4½"	8⅜"
6"	8½"	5⅛"	9¾"
7"	9⅞"	5⅞"	11⅛"
8"	11⅜"	6⅝"	12⅝"

Quilt Plans

As I worked on these different approaches to quilt design, one idea often led to another. I have a particular affection for patchwork cows, and I was determined to create a paper-pieced Cow block. Of course, a cow needs a barn, and the barn should have a house. The house needs a town, so the church, store, school, and apartment complex soon followed.

After I grouped the block designs for this book, I began to play with them to create a variety of quilts. It was so easy to select a few appropriate blocks to fit a design concept or theme and see what developed when I combined blocks and block sections.

Each Quilt Plan indicates the block layout and cut sizes of the setting pieces and borders.

One of the wonderful options that paper piecing affords is the ability to make blocks in a variety of sizes from the same design. All that is necessary is to photocopy the block in a reduced or enlarged size. See "Enlarging and Reducing Block Designs" on page 6. In order to demonstrate this option and some of the design possibilities it offers, the sample quilts in the gallery were made using a variety of block sizes.

Make photocopies of the quilt plan so you can experiment with different color schemes. Refer to the color photograph of the quilt or create a quilt using your own color combinations.

Each block design, variation, size, and color combination is assigned a letter. When a variation of a block design is used, the appropriate seam line(s) have been eliminated or added to the block illustration. See "Eliminating and Adding Seam Lines" on page 60. When the reverse of a block design is used, it is indicated. See "Creating the Reverse of a Block Design" on page 7.

The Block Placement Guide indicates the placement of each block design and color variations in the sample quilt.

A	A	A	A	A	A
A	C			C	A
A		B	B		A
A		B	B		A
A	C			C	A
A	A	A	A	A	A

Block Placement Guide

Yardage

The yardage estimates for the sample quilts have been calculated generously to allow for oversize cutting. When small amounts of the same fabric are used several times in the quilt, a ⅛ yard minimum is given.

The measurements given for borders and fabric pieces in the quilt plans are cut size. Cut larger pieces of fabric, such as those for setting squares, lattices, borders, corner squares, and binding first. Use the remainder of the fabric to piece the blocks. Yardage for borders and binding has been calculated for strips cut across the width of the fabric (crosswise grain) unless otherwise noted. Bindings are all constructed from 2"-wide strips.

Scrap pieces of fabric work well with these little paper-pieced patchwork blocks. Often a variety of scraps totaling an exact yardage in a particular color is specified so that you will have a sense of how much fabric is needed.

Down on the Farm

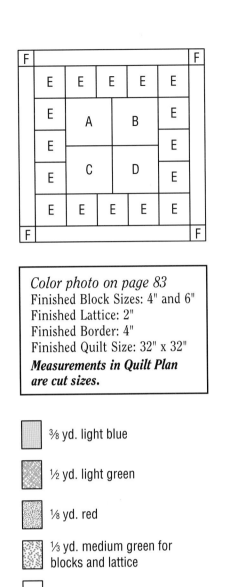

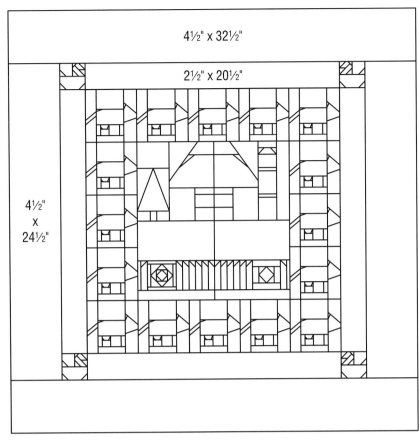

4½" x 32½"

2½" x 20½"

4½"
x
24½"

Color photo on page 83
Finished Block Sizes: 4" and 6"
Finished Lattice: 2"
Finished Border: 4"
Finished Quilt Size: 32" x 32"
**Measurements in Quilt Plan
are cut sizes.**

 ⅜ yd. light blue

 ½ yd. light green

⅛ yd. red

⅓ yd. medium green for
blocks and lattice

⅛ yd. white

⅛ yd. total assorted solid-
color scraps (mini quilts)

⅛ yd. black

⅛ yd. beige

⅛ yd. yellow

⅓ yd. black and white print

⅞ yd. medium blue for
border and binding

1 yd. for backing

36" x 36" piece of batting

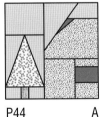

P44   A
Make 1
6" block†

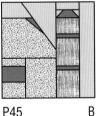

P45   B
Make 1
6" block†

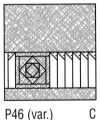

P46 (var.)   C
Make 1
6" block†

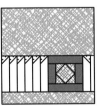

P47 (var.)   D
Reverse Block
Make 1
6" block†

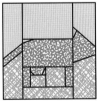

P33   E
Make 16
4" block

F   F

Bottom half only of
the 4" block P29
Make two sets

† *Enlarge block design to 6".*

Wedding Flower Rings

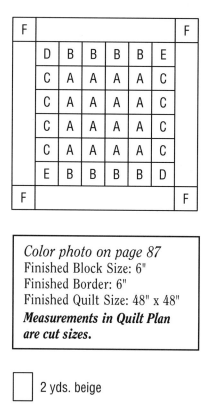

F					F
D	B	B	B	B	E
C	A	A	A	A	C
C	A	A	A	A	C
C	A	A	A	A	C
C	A	A	A	A	C
E	B	B	B	B	D
F					F

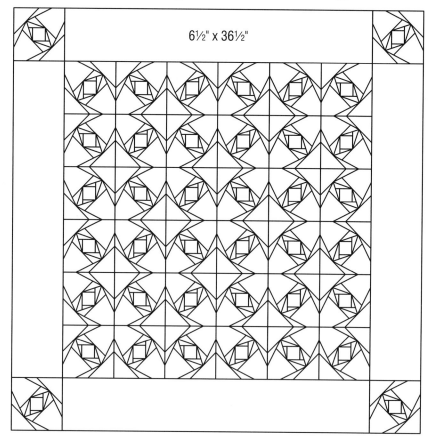

6½" x 36½"

Color photo on page 87
Finished Block Size: 6"
Finished Border: 6"
Finished Quilt Size: 48" x 48"
Measurements in Quilt Plan are cut sizes.

 2 yds. beige

2¼ yds. dark green for blocks, border and binding

¼ yd. total dark red scraps

¼ yd. total medium red scraps

¼ yd. total dark blue scraps

¼ yd. total medium blue scraps

⅜ yd. medium green

2⅞ yds. for backing

52" x 52" piece of batting

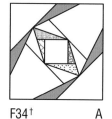

F34 †   A
Make 16

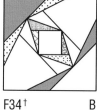

F34 †   B
Make 8

F34 †   C
Make 8

F34 †   D
Make 2

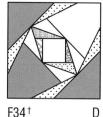

F34 †   E
Make 2

F34 †   F
Make 4

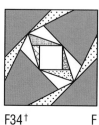

† *Enlarge block design to 6".*

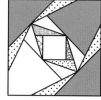

66   Quilt Plans

Garden Weave

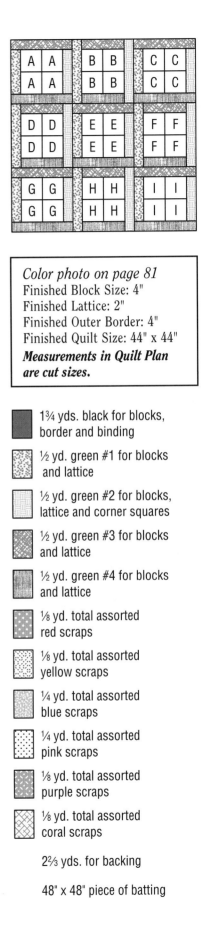

4½" x 36½"
← 4½" x 4½"
2½" x 12½"
2½" x 8½"

Color photo on page 81
Finished Block Size: 4"
Finished Lattice: 2"
Finished Outer Border: 4"
Finished Quilt Size: 44" x 44"
**Measurements in Quilt Plan
are cut sizes.**

1¾ yds. black for blocks,
border and binding

½ yd. green #1 for blocks
and lattice

½ yd. green #2 for blocks,
lattice and corner squares

½ yd. green #3 for blocks
and lattice

½ yd. green #4 for blocks
and lattice

⅛ yd. total assorted
red scraps

⅛ yd. total assorted
yellow scraps

¼ yd. total assorted
blue scraps

¼ yd. total assorted
pink scraps

⅛ yd. total assorted
purple scraps

⅛ yd. total assorted
coral scraps

2⅔ yds. for backing

48" x 48" piece of batting

F44   A
Make 4

F38   B
Make 4

F42   C
Make 4

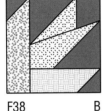

F41   D
Make 4

F43   E
Make 4

F45   F
Make 4

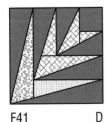

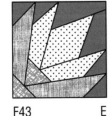

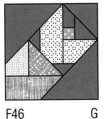

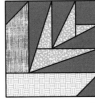

F46   G
Make 4

F40   H
Make 4

F39   I
Make 4

How Does Your Garden Grow?

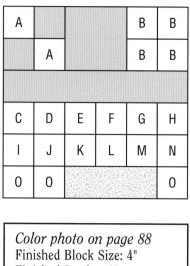

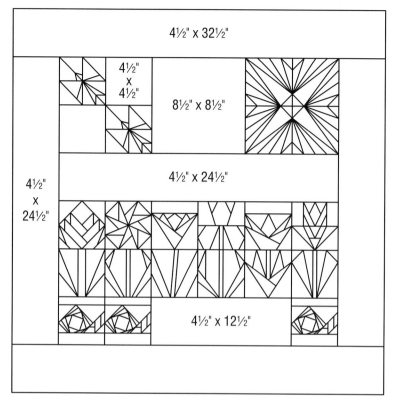

4½" x 32½"

4½" x 4½"

8½" x 8½"

4½" x 24½"

4½" x 24½"

4½" x 12½"

Color photo on page 88
Finished Block Size: 4"
Finished Border: 4"
Finished Quilt Size: 32" x 32"
**Measurements in Quilt Plan
are cut sizes.**

 ¾ yd. light blue for blocks
and setting pieces

 ¼ yd. total assorted
green fabrics

 ¼ yd. total assorted
yellow fabrics

 ⅛ yd. total assorted
purple fabrics

 ⅛ yd. total assorted
blue fabrics

 ⅛ yd. total assorted
pink fabrics

¼ yd. total assorted
brown fabrics

¼ yd. light green for blocks
and setting pieces

⅞ yd. for border and
binding

1 yd. for backing

36" x 36" piece of batting

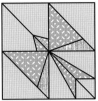

P13   A
Make 2

G32   B
Make 4

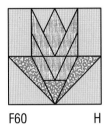

F58   C
Make 1

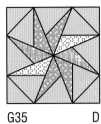

G35   D
Make 1

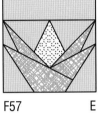

F57   E
Make 1

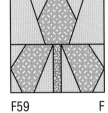

F59   F
Make 1

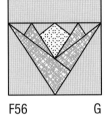

F56   G
Make 1

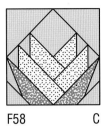

F60   H
Make 1

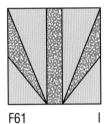

F61   I
Make 1

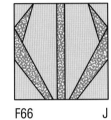

F66   J
Make 1

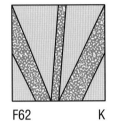

F62   K
Make 1

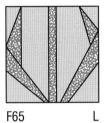

F65   L
Make 1

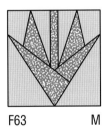

F63   M
Make 1

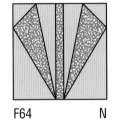

F64   N
Make 1

P31   O
Make 3

I'll Fly Away

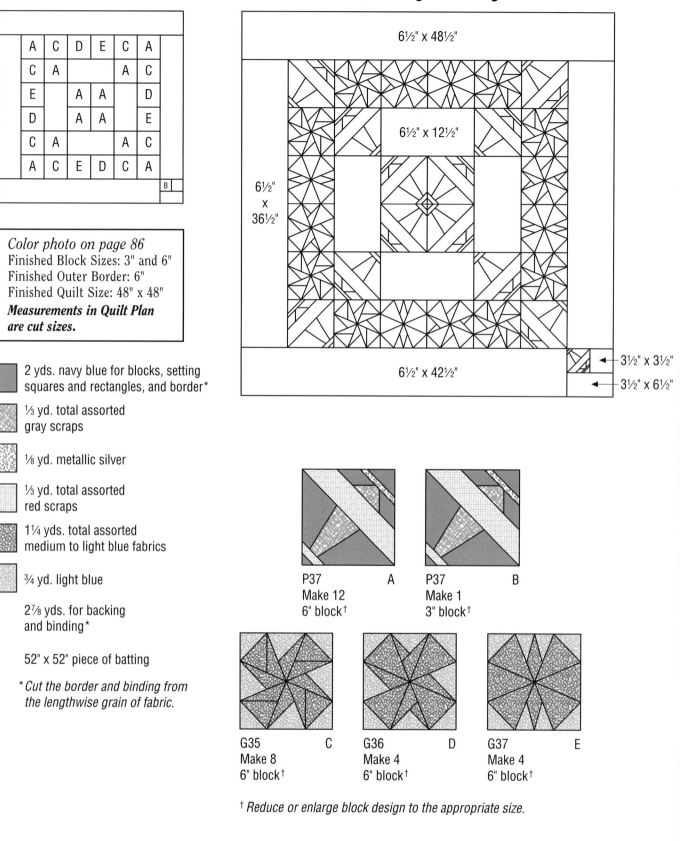

A	C	D	E	C	A
C	A			A	C
E		A	A		D
D		A	A		E
C	A			A	C
A	C	E	D	C	A

B

Color photo on page 86
Finished Block Sizes: 3" and 6"
Finished Outer Border: 6"
Finished Quilt Size: 48" x 48"
**Measurements in Quilt Plan
are cut sizes.**

2 yds. navy blue for blocks, setting squares and rectangles, and border*

⅓ yd. total assorted gray scraps

⅛ yd. metallic silver

⅓ yd. total assorted red scraps

1¼ yds. total assorted medium to light blue fabrics

¾ yd. light blue

2⅞ yds. for backing and binding*

52" x 52" piece of batting

Cut the border and binding from the lengthwise grain of fabric.

6½" x 48½"

6½" x 12½"

6½" x 36½"

6½" x 42½"

3½" x 3½"

3½" x 6½"

P37
Make 12
6" block†
A

P37
Make 1
3" block†
B

G35
Make 8
6" block†
C

G36
Make 4
6" block†
D

G37
Make 4
6" block†
E

† *Reduce or enlarge block design to the appropriate size.*

Iris Medallion

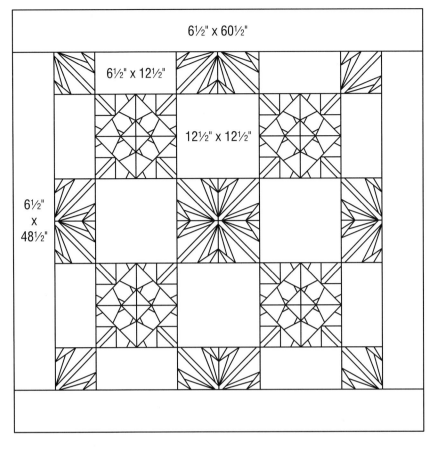

6½" x 60½"

6½" x 12½"

12½" x 12½"

6½"
x
48½"

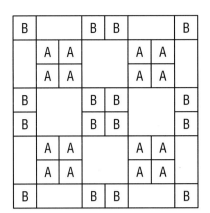

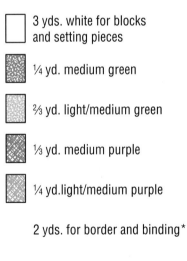

Color photo on page 87
Finished Block Size: 6"
Finished Border: 6"
Finished Quilt Size: 60" x 60"
**Measurements in Quilt Plan
are cut sizes.**

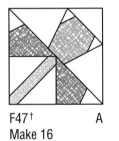

F47 †   A
Make 16

F50 †   B
Make 16

† *Enlarge block design to 6".*

☐ 3 yds. white for blocks
and setting pieces

▨ ¼ yd. medium green

▨ ⅔ yd. light/medium green

▨ ⅓ yd. medium purple

▨ ¼ yd. light/medium purple

2 yds. for border and binding*

3¾ yds. for backing

64" x 64" piece of batting

* *Cut the border and binding from
the lengthwise grain of fabric.*

It's Raining Cats and Dogs!

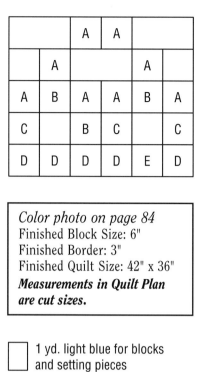

		A	A		
	A			A	
A	B	A	A	B	A
C		B	C		C
D	D	D	D	E	D

Color photo on page 84
Finished Block Size: 6"
Finished Border: 3"
Finished Quilt Size: 42" x 36"
**Measurements in Quilt Plan
are cut sizes.**

☐ 1 yd. light blue for blocks
and setting pieces

▦ ¾ yd. total solid
rainbow-color* scraps

▨ ⅛ yd. metallic silver

■ ⅛ yd. brown

▦ ⅛ yd. gray

▦ ¼ yd. total yellow
print scraps

1¼ yds. dark blue for
border and binding**

1¼ yds. for backing

46" x 46" piece of batting

*Red, orange, yellow, green,
blue and purple

**Cut the border and binding from
the lengthwise grain of fabric.

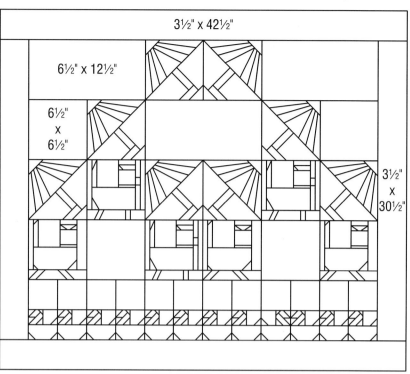

3½" x 42½"

6½" x 12½"

6½" x 6½"

3½" x 30½"

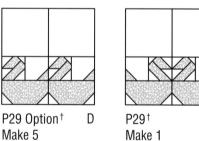

P36†   A
Make 8

P34†   B
Make 3

P35†   C
Make 3

P29 Option†   D
Make 5

P29†   E
Make 1

† Enlarge block design to 6".

Night Blooms

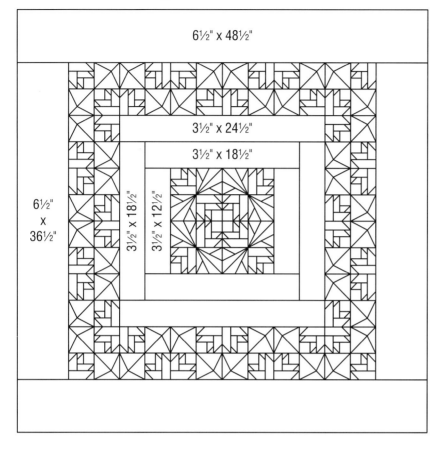

6½" x 48½"

3½" x 24½"

3½" x 18½"

3½" x 18½"

3½" x 12½"

6½" x 36½"

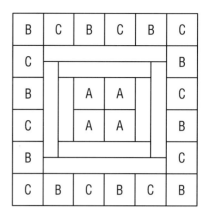

B	C	B	C	B	C
C					B
B		A	A		C
C		A	A		B
B					C
C	B	C	B	C	B

Color photo on page 85
Finished Block Size: 6"
Finished Inner Borders: 3"
Finished Outer Border: 6"
Finished Quilt Size: 48" x 48"
Measurements in Quilt Plan
are cut sizes.

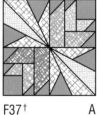

F37†
Make 4   A

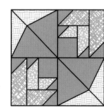

F36†
Make 10   B

F36†
Make 10   C

† *Enlarge block design to 6".*

■ 1½ yds. black

▨ ⅜ yd. light green for blocks
and second inner border

□ ¾ yd. medium green

□ ¼ yd. light purple

▨ ½ yd. medium purple

▨ ½ yd. dark purple

2 yds. dark green first inner border,
outer border and binding*

2⅞ yds. for backing

52" x 52" piece of batting

* *Cut the border and binding from
the lengthwise grain of fabric.*

Poinsettia Galaxy

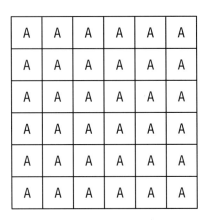

A	A	A	A	A	A
A	A	A	A	A	A
A	A	A	A	A	A
A	A	A	A	A	A
A	A	A	A	A	A
A	A	A	A	A	A

Color photo on page 86
Finished Block Size: 6"
Finished Border: 6"
Finished Quilt Size: 48" x 48"
**Measurements in Quilt Plan
are cut sizes.**

 ½ yd. dark red

3/8 yd. medium red

¾ yd. dark green

¾ yd. medium green

¾ yd. light green

 2½ yds. black for blocks,
border and binding*

2⅞ yds. for backing

52" x 52" piece of batting

* *Cut the border and binding from
the lengthwise grain of fabric.*

6½" x 48½"

6½"
x
36½"

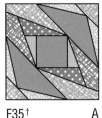

F35 †   A
Make 36

† *Enlarge block design to 6".*

Southern Cross

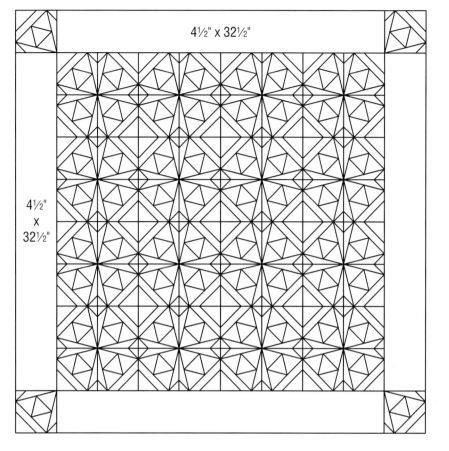

4½" x 32½"

4½"
x
32½"

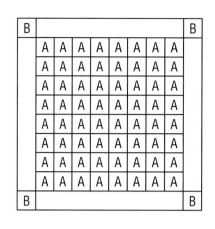

B | | | | | | | | B
A A A A A A A A
A A A A A A A A
A A A A A A A A
A A A A A A A A
A A A A A A A A
A A A A A A A A
A A A A A A A A
A A A A A A A A
B | | | | | | | | B

Color photo on page 82
Finished Block Size: 4"
Finished Border: 4"
Finished Quilt Size: 40" x 40"
**Measurements in Quilt Plan
are cut sizes.**

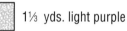 1⅓ yds. light purple

1¼ yds. black for blocks
and binding

¾ yd. dark purple for blocks
and border

1 yd. medium purple

1¼ yds. for backing

44" x 44" piece of batting

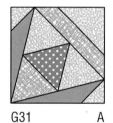

G31   A
Make 64

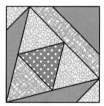

G31   B
Make 4

Spring Nosegays

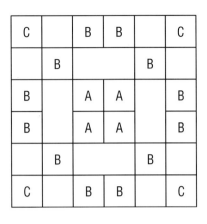

C		B	B		C
	B			B	
B		A	A		B
B		A	A		B
	B			B	
C		B	B		C

Color photo on page 88
Finished Block Size: 4"
Finished Inner Border: 2"
Finished Outer Border: 4"
Finished Quilt Size: 36" x 36"
Measurements in Quilt Plan are cut sizes.

1 yd. white for blocks and setting pieces

 ½ yd. total assorted green scraps

 ¼ yd. total assorted colored-fabric scraps

⅓ yd. medium pink for inner border

⅞ yd. green for outer border and binding

1⅛ yds. for backing

40" x 40" piece of batting

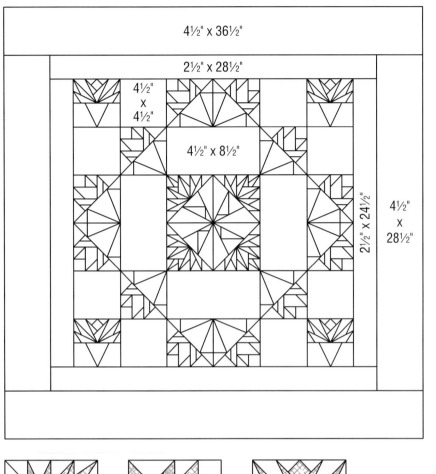

4½" x 36½"

2½" x 28½"

4½" x 4½"

4½" x 8½"

2½" x 24½"

4½" x 28½"

F68   A
Make 4

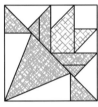

F67   B
Make 12

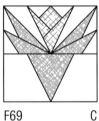

F69   C
Make 4

The Aquatic Community

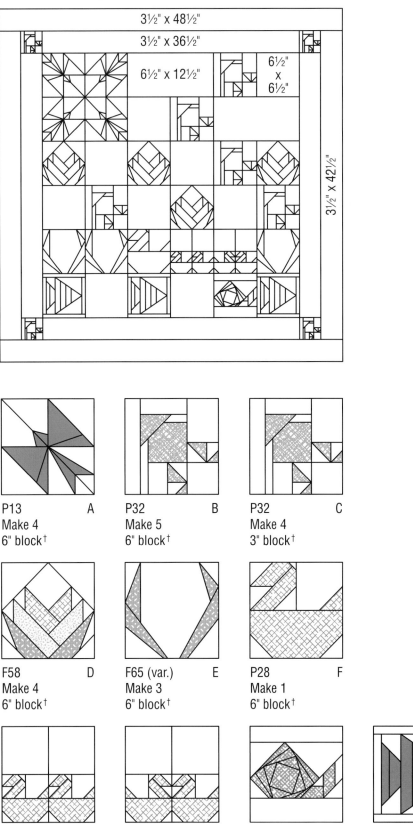

3½" x 48½"

3½" x 36½"

6½" x 12½"

6½" x 6½"

3½" x 42½"

C					C
A	A			B	
A	A		B		
D		D		B	D
	B		D		B
E	E	F	G	H	E
J		J		I	J
C					C

Color photo on page 83
Finished Block Sizes: 3" and 6"
Finished Inner Border: 3"
Finished Outer Border: 3"
Finished Quilt Size: 48" x 48"
Measurements in Quilt Plan are cut sizes.

□ 2¼ yds. light blue for blocks, squares, rectangles and inner border

▨ ¼ yd. green (frogs)

▨ ¼ yd. total assorted green scraps

▨ ¼ yd. total assorted yellow scraps

▨ ⅛ yd. white

▨ ⅛ yd. total assorted brown scraps

▨ ⅓ yd. total assorted solid rainbow-color* scraps

1½ yds. green for outer border and binding**

2⅞ yds. for backing

52" x 52" piece of batting

*Red, orange, yellow, green, blue and purple

**Cut the border and binding from the lengthwise grain of fabric.

P13   A
Make 4
6" block†

P32   B
Make 5
6" block†

P32   C
Make 4
3" block†

F58   D
Make 4
6" block†

F65 (var.)   E
Make 3
6" block†

P28   F
Make 1
6" block†

P29 Option   G
Make 1
6" block†

P29   H
Make 1
6" block†

P31   I
Make 1
6" block†

P30   J
Make 3
6" block†

† Reduce or enlarge block design to the appropriate size.

Town and Country

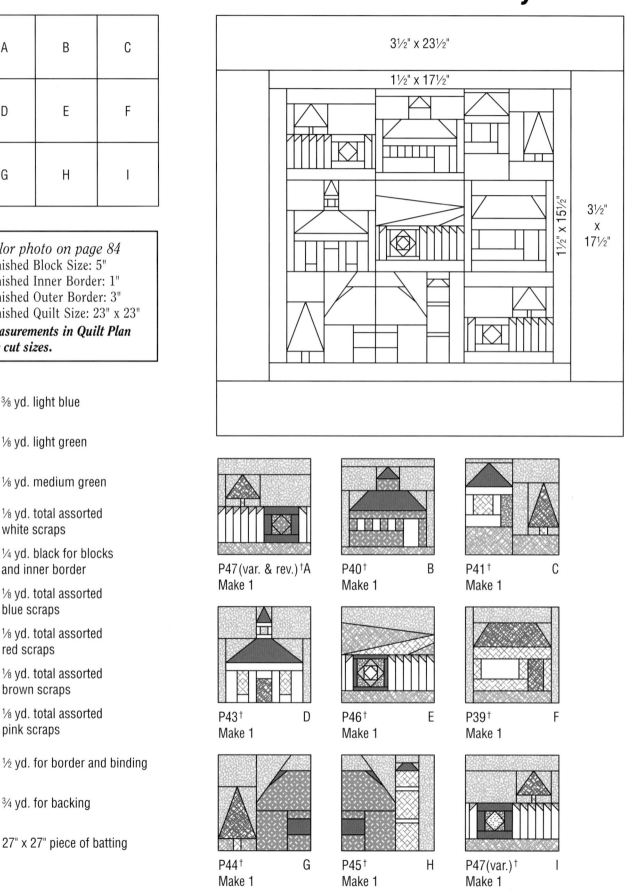

3½" x 23½"

1½" x 17½"

1½" x 15½"

3½" x 17½"

Color photo on page 84
Finished Block Size: 5"
Finished Inner Border: 1"
Finished Outer Border: 3"
Finished Quilt Size: 23" x 23"
Measurements in Quilt Plan are cut sizes.

 ⅜ yd. light blue

 ⅛ yd. light green

 ⅛ yd. medium green

⅛ yd. total assorted white scraps

¼ yd. black for blocks and inner border

 ⅛ yd. total assorted blue scraps

 ⅛ yd. total assorted red scraps

 ⅛ yd. total assorted brown scraps

 ⅛ yd. total assorted pink scraps

½ yd. for border and binding

¾ yd. for backing

27" x 27" piece of batting

P47(var. & rev.) †A
Make 1

P40 †   B
Make 1

P41 †   C
Make 1

P43 †   D
Make 1

P46 †   E
Make 1

P39 †   F
Make 1

P44 †   G
Make 1

P45 †   H
Make 1

P47(var.) †   I
Make 1

† *Enlarge block design to 5".*

Unchained Melody

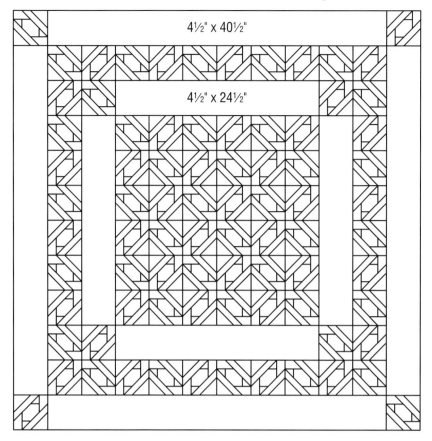

4½" x 40½"

4½" x 24½"

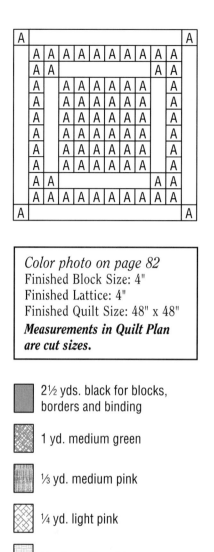

Color photo on page 82
Finished Block Size: 4"
Finished Lattice: 4"
Finished Quilt Size: 48" x 48"
**Measurements in Quilt Plan
are cut sizes.**

2½ yds. black for blocks,
borders and binding

1 yd. medium green

⅓ yd. medium pink

¼ yd. light pink

⅓ yd. medium blue

¼ yd. light blue

2⅞ yds. for backing

52" x 52" piece of batting

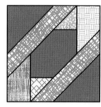

F32   A
Make 80

Windblown Rose

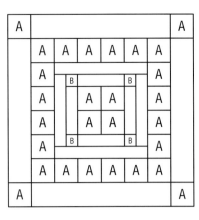

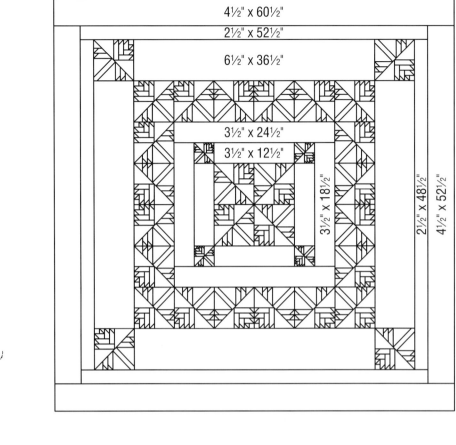

4½" x 60½"
2½" x 52½"
6½" x 36½"
3½" x 24½"
3½" x 12½"
3½" x 18½"
2½" x 48½"
4½" x 52½"

Color photo on page 85
Finished Block Sizes: 3" and 6"
Finished Beige Border
   and Lattice: 3" and 6"
Finished Outer Medium
   Red Border: 2"
Finished Outer
   Dark Green Border: 4"
Finished Quilt Size: 60" x 60"
**Measurements in Quilt Plan
are cut sizes.**

 3½ yds. beige for blocks, inner border and lattice

 ⅓ yd. dark red

 ⅓ yd. medium dark red

1½ yds. medium red for blocks and 2" border*

2¼ yds. dark green for blocks, outer border and binding*

⅓ yd. medium dark green

 ½ yd. medium green

3¾ yds. for backing

64" x 64" piece of batting

Cut the border and binding from the lengthwise grain of fabric.

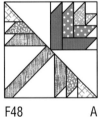

F48   A
Make 28
6" block†

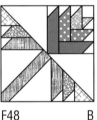

F48   B
Make 4
3" block†

† *Reduce or enlarge block design
  to the appropriate size.*

 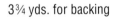

Gallery of Quilts

Garden Weave by Carol Doak, 1994, Windham, New Hampshire, 44" x 44". This colorful scrap quilt combines nine different paper-pieced designs, resulting in dramatic radiating floral patterns. The alternating long and short sides of the blocks appear to be woven.

Southern Cross by Helen Weinman, 1994, Centerville, Massachusetts, 40" x 40". Just one rotated Geometric block design creates this wonderful pattern. The black fabric, combined with shades of purple, creates a radiating pattern that appears to be set on point with alternating small squares.

Unchained Melody by Carol Doak, 1994, Windham, New Hampshire, 48" x 48". This dramatic medallion quilt uses just one nine-piece Floral block design. The medium and light fabrics set against the black background make a bold statement.

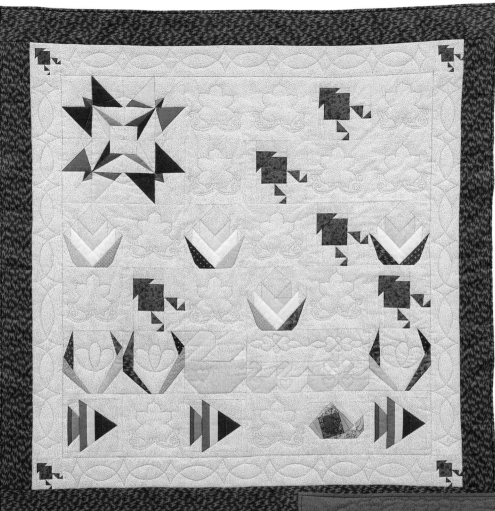

The Aquatic Community (above) by Ginny Guaraldi, 1994, Londonderry, New Hampshire, 48" x 48". Picture and Flower block designs make up this whimsical scene. One baby duck is already displaying his independent nature!

Down on the Farm (right) by Carol Doak, 1994, Windham, New Hampshire, 32" x 32". This cheery little scenic medallion wall quilt combines a herd of paper-pieced cows and Barn blocks. Obviously a quilter lives "down on this farm," because she is airing her 2¼" pieced quilts!

It's Raining Cats and Dogs (above) by Terry Maddox, 1994, Pelham, New Hampshire, 42" x 36". The inspiration for this project came from its title and resulted in a cheery little quilt that is sure to delight any child. Rainbow-colored umbrellas shield the cats and dogs, who are unaware of the river of ducks below.

Town and Country (right) by Carol Doak, 1994, Windham, New Hampshire, 23" x 23". A variety of scenic Picture blocks produce a miniature wall quilt with lots of detail. The three tiny pieced quilts airing on the picket fences are only 2¼" square.

Night Blooms by Ellen B. Peters, 1994, Laconia, New Hampshire, 48" x 48". A diagonal Flower block creates a dramatic border around the center of this quilt. The rich greens and purples against the black background and the intricate quilting design worked in silver metallic thread provide an exotic flavor.

Windblown Rose by Susan L. Raban, 1995, Nashua, New Hampshire, 60" x 60". This delicate Flower block has an "old time" flavor. It spins about the center of the quilt, setting in motion an elegant medallion-style quilt design. The red and green fabrics in three shades and the small Flower blocks provide delightful detail, which is accented by the soft curves of the quilting in the borders.

Poinsettia Galaxy *(above) by Sherry Reis, 1994, Worthington, Ohio, 48" x 48". Just one Flower block with two diagonal design elements creates this spectacular quilt. The combination of the intricate design and the intense colors set against a black background not only captivates, but demands, your complete attention.*

I'll Fly Away *(right) by B. J. Berlo, 1994, Auburn, New Hampshire, 48" x 48". The Airplane blocks radiate from the center of this quilt and fly around the perimeter. A smaller plane has its own flight plan! The Kaleidoscope blocks create a border of whirling propellers to complete this medallion-style quilt. B. J. worked for an airline for twenty-six years and has done a lot of "flying away."*

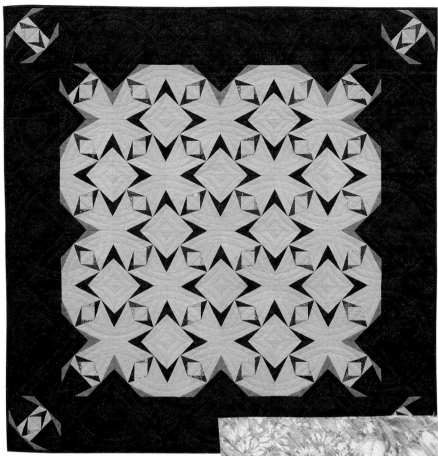

Wedding Flower Rings by Sherry Reis, 1994, Worthington, Ohio, 48" x 48". Different fabric placements in the same Flower block design results in an intricate pieced pattern with scalloped edges. Sherry used a double wedding ring quilting pattern to accentuate the interlocking circles.

Iris Medallion by Pam Ludwig, 1994, Windham, New Hampshire, 60" x 60". The diagonal Iris block and a diagonal Leaf block team up in this medallion-style quilt to make a pretty floral quilt. The multicolor print border ties it all together perfectly.

How Does Your Garden Grow? by Carol Doak, 1994, Windham, New Hampshire, 32" x 32". Several vertical flower tops are teamed up with vertical flower stem-and-leaf bottoms to create a flower garden. Four glitzy Geometric blocks radiate a warm sunshine where butterflies and even snails are right at home.

Spring Nosegays by Carol Doak, 1994, Windham, New Hampshire, 36" x 36". Three different Nosegay blocks are used in this small medallion scrap quilt that is sure to brighten any room.

Quilt Finishing

Joining Blocks

Arrange the blocks and setting pieces as shown in the block placement guide for the quilt you are making. To join blocks, place them right sides together and match the intersecting seam lines. Pin through the seam lines of both blocks and stitch along the marked line. Before sewing the seam, I machine baste the beginning of the block, any points that must match, and the end of the block. Once the seam is machine basted, open it for a quick check to make sure the seams align correctly. If they do, proceed to sew the seam. If they don't quite match, remove the machine basting and try again. Basting at these crucial matching points also secures them so they won't shift while you sew. Machine basting takes just a few minutes but eliminates a lot of frustration.

■ **Tip:** Place a block with points at the outside edge so that the points face up as you sew the seam. This way, you will be sure you are sewing across the point and not through it. If both blocks have points, have faith!

Press the seams in opposite directions from row to row. Pressing in this manner will lock the seams into a good match. Sew the rows together, making sure to match the seams between each block.

■ **Tip:** If the outside edges of your blocks are mostly one fabric color, change the thread to match.

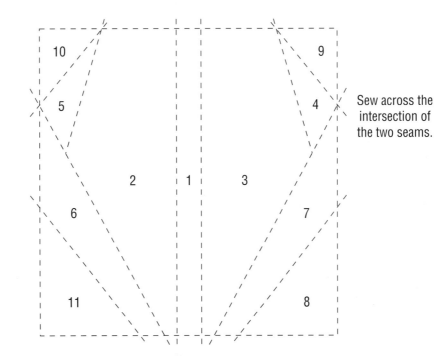

Sew across the intersection of the two seams.

Adding Borders

The quilts in this book have borders with straight-cut corners. Some of them have straight-cut borders with corner squares.

Straight-Cut Corners

1. Measure the length of the quilt top at the center, from raw edge to raw edge, and cut two border strips to that measurement. Mark the center of the border strips and the sides of the quilt top. Join the borders to the sides, matching center marks and edges. Ease as necessary. Press the seams toward the borders.

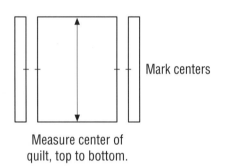

Mark centers

Measure center of
quilt, top to bottom.

2. Measure the width of the quilt top through the center, from raw edge to raw edge, including the border pieces just added. Cut two border strips to that measurement. Mark the centers of the border strips and the center top and center bottom of the quilt top. Join the border strips to the top and bottom edges, matching centers and ends and easing as necessary. Press the seams toward the borders.

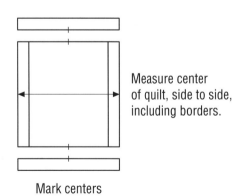

Measure center
of quilt, side to side,
including borders.

Mark centers

Borders with Corner Squares

1. Measure and cut border strips to match all four sides of the quilt top. Sew border strips to 2 opposite sides of the quilt top; press the seams toward the borders.

2. Attach the corner-square blocks to both ends of the remaining top and bottom border strips and press the seams toward the border strips. Sew these strips to the top and bottom edges of the quilt top, matching centers, seams, and ends. Ease as necessary. Press the seams toward the borders.

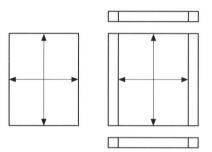

Removing Paper and Pressing Blocks

Remove the paper only after the completed blocks have been joined to other blocks, fabric pieces, or borders. Give a slight tug against the seam to loosen the paper from the stitching. Use a small pair of tweezers to remove pieces of paper left behind. Don't concern yourself with removing every tiny piece of paper caught under the stitches. They will only add warmth to the quilt! As you remove the paper, admire the wonderfully accurate blocks you have made with paper piecing.

Once the paper has been removed, press the blocks gently with a dry iron, using an up-and-down motion. Dragging a steam iron across the blocks distorts them.

Basting the Quilt

Once the paper has been removed, you can sandwich and baste the top. The sandwich consists of the backing, batting, and quilt top. There are many types of quilt batting available. Use a thin, low-loft batting for small wall quilts—they don't need to keep the wall warm. The low-loft batting also helps you to take smaller stitches when quilting the smaller-scale designs. Cut the backing and batting 2" to 3" larger than the quilt top all around.

1. Spread the backing, wrong side up, on a clean surface. Use masking tape or large binder clamps to anchor the backing to the table, being careful not to stretch it out of shape.
2. Spread and smooth the quilt batting over the backing. Make sure it covers the entire backing.
3. Place the quilt top on top of the batting, right side up, smoothing out any wrinkles. Make sure the edges of the quilt top are parallel to the edges of the backing.

4. Beginning in the center and working to the outside edges, make diagonal, vertical, and horizontal rows of basting stitches in a grid. (If you plan to machine quilt, you may choose to pin baste with size 2, rustproof safety pins.)

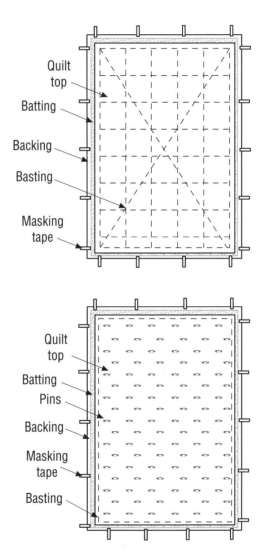

5. Bring the edge of the backing around to the front of the quilt top and baste in place in order to contain any exposed batting while quilting.

Quilting the Quilt

Quilt your projects by hand or machine, or use a combination of both. If you prefer hand quilting, keep in mind that piecing tiny blocks does not leave a large amount of single-layer fabric available for hand quilting, so plan accordingly. You might want to alternate solid squares and/or add plain fabric borders to showcase your hand quilting. On the other hand, it's easy to machine quilt small projects made of miniature blocks. If you use a polyester batting that requires quilting intervals every 3" to 4", your paper-pieced project utilizing 4" blocks will not require a large amount of quilting.

One of my friends who machine quilts, Helen Weinman, discovered how to use the paper-pieced patterns as a guide for machine quilting a similar design on her quilt. Helen simply photocopies one of the paper-pieced designs, pins the paper pattern to the quilt, and machine quilts the shape she desires through the paper. Once the machine quilting is complete, she tears the paper away from the stitching.

Begin quilting the project in the middle and work toward the edges in a consistent fashion. It is similar to smoothing bubbles to the outside edge when wall papering.

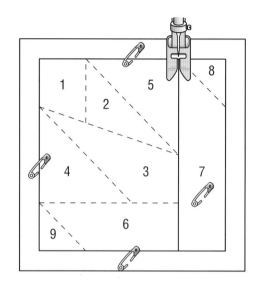

Binding the Edges

Once you have completed the quilting, prepare the quilt for binding by removing the basting stitches and trimming the batting and backing even with the edge of the quilt top. Adjust your machine for a basting-length stitch and use a walking foot or an even-feed foot, if available. Stitch around the perimeter of the quilt sandwich approximately ⅛" from the edge. The even-feed foot aids in sewing all three layers smoothly. If you are adding a sleeve to hang your quilt project, baste it in place now. (See page 94.)

Because the edges of wall quilts do not receive stress from handling, I prefer to use binding that has been cut on the straight of grain. I use fabric strips cut on the bias when binding bed quilts because bias strips are stronger and do not wear as quickly as straight-grain strips.

To make straight-grain binding:

1. Cut strips 2" wide across the width of the fabric (crosswise grain). Seam the ends at a 45° angle to make a strip long enough to go around the outside edges of the quilt, plus about 10". Trim excess fabric and press seams open.

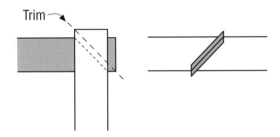

2. Fold the strip in half lengthwise, wrong sides together, and press.

3. Place the binding on the front of the quilt, lining up the raw edges of the binding with the raw edges of the quilt. Using a walking foot, if possible, sew

the binding to the quilt, using a ¼"-wide seam. Leave the first few inches of the binding loose so that you can join the beginning and ending of the binding strip later.

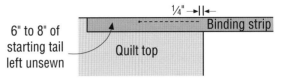

4. Stop stitching ¼" from the corner of the quilt and backstitch. Turn the quilt to sew the next edge. To make a mitered corner, fold the binding up and away from the quilt and then down, even with the next side. The straight fold should be even with the top edge of the quilt. Stitch from the edge to the next corner, stopping ¼" from the corner. Repeat for the remaining corners.

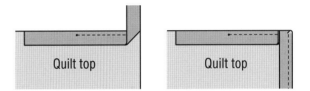

5. As you approach the beginning of the binding, stop and overlap the binding ½" from the start of the binding strip and trim the excess. Open the folds of the two strips and sew the ends together with a ¼"-wide seam allowance. Press the seam allowance open. Return the seamed strip to the edge and finish the seam.

6. Fold the binding to the back over the raw edges of the quilt. The folded edge of the binding should cover the machine-stitching line. Blindstitch the binding in place.

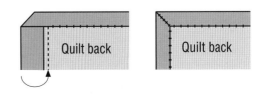

Adding a Sleeve

The preferred method for hanging a wall quilt is to slip a rod through a sleeve that has been sewn on the back of the quilt. You can use the same fabric as the backing so it will blend in, or simply use a piece of muslin.

1. Cut a 6"- to 8"-wide strip of fabric as long as the top of the quilt. Hem both ends of the strip.

2. Fold the strip, wrong sides together, and pin the raw edges at the top of the quilt before attaching the binding. Machine baste in place ⅛" from the edge. Add the binding to the quilt as described on page 93.

3. Blindstitch the folded edge of the sleeve to the back of the quilt.

Signing Your Work

Your quilt is an expression of you. Be sure to make a label for the back of the quilt, containing information such as your name, the date the quilt was completed, the name of the quilt, your town, the recipient of a gift quilt, and any other information you would like to add. I, as well as many of my friends, have adopted the delightful option of using a paper-pieced block as a label. Write on the block with a permanent-ink marking pen.

I now piece the label for my quilts after completing all the blocks for the quilt top. I usually choose one of the patterns used on the front of the quilt and make it while the fabrics are handy. Use plain fabrics in the areas where you will write information. Before I begin to piece the block, I trim the paper pattern on the finished outside line. When the block is complete, I trim the fabrics around the outside edge to ¼" from the edge, press over the edge of the paper, and pin in place. If there are a lot of seams at the outside edge, you can add small strips of fabric to frame the block. If you prefer this option, do *not* trim the paper pattern on the finished outside line. Treat it as you would normally treat your paper-pieced blocks and trim them ¼" from the outside line. Just before attaching the label, remove the pins and paper. Pin the block label on the back of the quilt and blindstitch it in place.

Meet the Author

Carol Doak is an award-winning quiltmaker, author, and teacher. She began her teaching career in 1980, in Worthington, Ohio. Carol's teaching has taken her to many cities in the United States and recently to Australia to share her quiltmaking "Tricks of the Trade." She writes a column of the same title for *Quick and Easy Quilting* magazine. Her lighthearted approach and ability to teach have earned her high marks and positive comments from workshop participants.

Carol's quilts have been presented in several books, such as *Great American Quilts 1990* and *The Quilt Encyclopedia*. She has been featured in several national quilt magazines, and her quilts have appeared on the covers of *Quilter's Newsletter Magazine, Quilt World, Quilting Today,* and *McCall's Quilting.*

Carol's first book, *Quiltmaker's Guide: Basics & Beyond,* was published in 1992. Her second book, *Country Medallion Sampler,* published in 1993, combines a medallion-style quilt with a country theme. Carol's third book, *EasyMachine Paper Piecing,* set in motion a passion for designing and creating foundation-pieced patchwork quilts. Carol used her paper-pieced block designs and quick foundation-piecing methods to create the garments featured in *Easy Reversible Vests.* Her latest book, *Easy Paper-Pieced Keepsake Quilts,* features more paper-pieced quilts to treasure.

Carol lives with her family in Windham, New Hampshire, where the snow-filled winter months provide a pretty picture to contemplate as she keeps cozy under quilts in progress.

That Patchwork Place Publications and Products

All the Blocks Are Geese by Mary Sue Suit
All New Copy Art for Quilters
All-Star Sampler by Roxanne Carter
Angle Antics by Mary Hickey
Animas Quilts by Jackie Robinson
Appliqué Borders: An Added Grace
    by Jeana Kimball
Appliqué in Bloom by Gabrielle Swain
Appliquilt™ for Christmas by Tonee White
Appliquilt™: Whimsical One-Step Appliqué
    by Tonee White
Appliquilt™ Your ABCs by Tonee White
Around the Block with Judy Hopkins
Baltimore Bouquets by Mimi Dietrich
Bargello Quilts by Marge Edie
Basic Beauties by Eileen Westfall
Basket Garden by Mary Hickey
Bias Square® Miniatures
    by Christine Carlson
Biblical Blocks by Rosemary Makhan
Block by Block by Beth Donaldson
Borders by Design by Paulette Peters
Botanical Wreaths by Laura M. Reinstatler
Calendar Quilts by Joan Hanson
The Calico House by Joanna Brazier
Cathedral Window: A Fresh Look
    by Nancy J. Martin
The Cat's Meow by Janet Kime
A Child's Garden of Quilts
    by Christal Carter
Colourwash Quilts by Deirdre Amsden
Corners in the Cabin by Paulette Peters
Country Medallion Sampler by Carol Doak
Country Threads by Connie Tesene and
    Mary Tendall
Decoupage Quilts by Barbara Roberts
Designing Quilts by Suzanne Hammond
The Easy Art of Appliqué
    by Mimi Dietrich & Roxi Eppler
Easy Machine Paper Piecing by Carol Doak
Easy Mix & Match Machine Paper Piecing
    by Carol Doak
Easy Paper-Pieced Keepsake Quilts
    by Carol Doak
Easy Quilts...By Jupiter!®
    by Mary Beth Maison
Easy Reversible Vests by Carol Doak
Fantasy Flowers
    by Doreen Cronkite Burbank
Five- and Seven-Patch Blocks & Quilts
    for the ScrapSaver by Judy Hopkins
Four-Patch Blocks & Quilts for the
    ScrapSaver by Judy Hopkins
Freedom in Design by Mia Rozmyn
Fun with Fat Quarters by Nancy J. Martin
Go Wild with Quilts by Margaret Rolfe

Handmade Quilts by Mimi Dietrich
Happy Endings by Mimi Dietrich
The Heirloom Quilt by Yolande Filson
    and Roberta Przybylski
In The Beginning by Sharon Evans Yenter
Irma's Sampler by Irma Eskes
Jacket Jazz by Judy Murrah
Jacket Jazz Encore by Judy Murrah
The Joy of Quilting by Joan Hanson and
    Mary Hickey
Le Rouvray by Diane de Obaldia,
    with Marie-Christine Flocard
    and Cosabeth Parriaud
Little Quilts by Alice Berg, Sylvia Johnson,
    and Mary Ellen Von Holt
Lively Little Logs by Donna McConnell
Loving Stitches by Jeana Kimball
Machine Quilting Made Easy
    by Maurine Noble
Make Room for Quilts by Nancy J. Martin
Nifty Ninepatches by Carolann M. Palmer
Nine-Patch Blocks & Quilts for the
    ScrapSaver by Judy Hopkins
Not Just Quilts by Jo Parrott
Oh! Christmas Trees
    compiled by Barbara Weiland
On to Square Two by Marsha McCloskey
Osage County Quilt Factory
    by Virginia Robertson
Our Pieceful Village by Lynn Rice
Painless Borders by Sally Schneider
Patchwork Basics by Marie-Christine
    Flocard & Cosabeth Parriaud
A Perfect Match by Donna Lynn Thomas
Picture Perfect Patchwork
    by Naomi Norman
Piecemakers® Country Store
    by the Piecemakers
A Pioneer Doll and Her Quilts
    by Mary Hickey
Pioneer Storybook Quilts by Mary Hickey
Prairie People—Cloth Dolls to Make
    and Cherish by Marji Hadley and
    J. Dianne Ridgley
Quick & Easy Quiltmaking by Mary Hickey,
    Nancy J. Martin, Marsha McCloskey
    and Sara Nephew
The Quilt Patch by Leslie Anne Pfeifer
The Quilt Room by Pam Lintott and
    Rosemary Miller
The Quilted Apple by Laurene Sinema
Quilted for Christmas
    compiled by Ursula Reikes
Quilted for Christmas, Book II
    compiled by Christine Barnes and
    Barbara Weiland

Quilted Sea Tapestries by Ginny Eckley
The Quilters' Companion
    compiled by That Patchwork Place
The Quilting Bee
    by Jackie Wolff and Lori Aluna
Quilting Makes the Quilt by Lee Cleland
Quilts for All Seasons by Christal Carter
Quilts for Baby: Easy as A, B, C
    by Ursula Reikes
Quilts for Kids by Carolann M. Palmer
Quilts from Nature by Joan Colvin
Quilts to Share by Janet Kime
Rotary Riot
    by Judy Hopkins and Nancy J. Martin
Rotary Roundup
    by Judy Hopkins and Nancy J. Martin
Round About Quilts by J. Michelle Watts
Round Robin Quilts
    by Pat Magaret and Donna Slusser
Samplings from the Sea
    by Rosemary Makhan
ScrapMania by Sally Schneider
Seasoned with Quilts by Retta Warehime
Sensational Settings by Joan Hanson
Sewing on the Line
    by Lesly-Claire Greenberg
Shortcuts: A Concise Guide to Rotary
    Cutting by Donna Lynn Thomas
Shortcuts Sampler by Roxanne Carter
Shortcuts to the Top
    by Donna Lynn Thomas
Small Talk by Donna Lynn Thomas
Smoothstitch® Quilts by Roxi Eppler
The Stitchin' Post
    by Jean Wells and Lawry Thorn
Stringing Along by Trice Boerens
Sunbonnet Sue All Through the Year
    by Sue Linker
Tea Party Time by Nancy J. Martin
Template-Free® Quiltmaking
    by Trudie Hughes
Template-Free® Quilts and Borders
    by Trudie Hughes
Template-Free® Stars by Jo Parrott
Through the Window & Beyond
    by Lynne Edwards
Treasures from Yesteryear, Book One
    by Sharon Newman
Treasures from Yesteryear, Book Two
    by Sharon Newman
Trouble Free Triangles by Gayle Bong
Two for Your Money by Jo Parrott
Watercolor Quilts
    by Pat Magaret and Donna Slusser
Woven & Quilted by Mary Anne Caplinger

4", 6", 8", & metric Bias Square® • BiRangle™ • Ruby Beholder™ • Pineapple Rule • ScrapMaster • Rotary Rule™ • Rotary Mate™
Shortcuts to America's Best-Loved Quilts (video)

Many titles are available at your local quilt shop. For more information, send $2 for a color catalog to
That Patchwork Place, Inc., PO Box 118, Bothell WA 98041-0118 USA.

☎ Call 1-800-426-3126 for the name and location of the quilt shop nearest you.